Alberto Manguel was born in  abroad since 1968 in France, It now settled in Canada. He is c *Places* (1980) which has been tr Japanese and Spanish and ed *Fantastic Literature* wh

OTHER FIRES

SHORT FICTION BY
LATIN AMERICAN WOMEN

Edited by Alberto Manguel

PICADOR

published by Pan Books

First published in the United States by Clarkson N. Potter, Inc. New York
First published in Great Britain 1986 by Pan Books Ltd,
Cavaye Place, London SW10 9PG
9 8 7 6 5 4 3 2
Selection, Introduction and Notes © Alberto Manguel 1986
English translation of stories by Silvina Ocampo, Alejandra
Pizarnik, Liliana Heker, Marta Lynch, Beatriz Guido, Vlady
Kociancich, Angélica Gorodischer, Amparo Dávila, Elena
Garro, Rosario Castellanos, Inés Arredondo, Armonía Somers
and Albalucía Angel, copyright © Alberto Manguel 1986.

ISBN 0 330 28827 X

Printed and bound in Great Britain by
Cox & Wyman Ltd, Reading

*This book is for
Ellin Slonitz,
who taught me to read
and for
Louise Dennys,
who taught me to write*

Acknowledgments

Every effort has been made to ensure that permissions for all materials acknowledged below were obtained. In the event of any inadvertent omissions, formal acknowledgments will be included in all future editions of this book.

Armonía Somers THE FALL, copyright © 1967 by Armonía Somers. Translation copyright © 1985 by Alberto Manguel.

Rachel de Queiroz METONYMY, OR THE HUSBAND'S REVENGE, copyright © 1958 by Rachel de Queiroz. Translation copyright © 1967 by William L. Grossman.

Marta Lynch LATIN LOVER, copyright © 1970 by Marta Lynch. Translation copyright © 1985 by Alberto Manguel.

Clarice Lispector THE IMITATION OF THE ROSE, copyright © 1955 by Clarice Lispector. Translation copyright © 1980 by Giovanni Pontiero.

Dinah Silveira de Queiroz GUIDANCE, copyright © 1949 by Dinah Silveira de Queiroz. Translation copyright © 1961 by William L. Grossman.

Alejandra Pizarnik THE BLOODY COUNTESS, copyright © 1968 by Alejandra Pizarnik. Translation copyright © 1985 by Alberto Manguel.

Angélica Gorodischer MAN'S DWELLING PLACE, copyright © 1968 by Angélica Gorodischer. Translation copyright © 1985 by Alberto Manguel.

Vlady Kociancich KNIGHT, DEATH AND THE DEVIL, copyright © 1968 by Vlady Kociancich. Translation copyright © 1985 by Alberto Manguel.

Inés Arredondo THE SHUNAMMITE, copyright © 1960 by Inés Arredondo. Translation copyright © 1985 by Alberto Manguel.

Albalucía Angel THE GUERRILLERO, copyright © 1979 by Albalucía Ángel. Translation copyright © 1985 by Alberto Manguel.

Amparo Dávila HAUTE CUISINE, copyright © 1972 by Amparo Dávila. Translation copyright © 1985 by Alberto Manguel.

Elena Poniatowska THE NIGHT VISITOR, copyright © 1985 by Elena Poniatowska. Translation copyright © 1985 by Catherine S. White-House.

Silvina Ocampo TWO REPORTS, copyright © 1967 by Silvina Ocampo. Translation copyright © 1985 by Alberto Manguel.

Liliana Heker THE STOLEN PARTY, copyright © 1982 by Liliana Heker. Translation copyright © 1985 by Alberto Manguel.

Elena Garro IT'S THE FAULT OF THE TLAXCALTECAS, copyright © 1965 by Elena Garro. Translation copyright © 1985 by Alberto Manguel.

Lygia Fagundes Telles TIGRELA, copyright © 1985 by Lygia Fagundes Telles. Translation copyright © 1985 by Eloah F. Giacomelli.

Beatriz Guido THE USURPER, copyright © 1980 by Beatriz Guido. Translation copyright © 1985 by Alberto Manguel.

Lydia Cabrera HOW THE MONKEY LOST THE FRUIT OF HIS LABOR, copyright © 1985 by Lydia Cabrera. Translation copyright © 1985 by Suzanne Jill Levine and Mary Caldwell.

Rosario Castellanos DEATH OF THE TIGER, copyright © 1960 by Rosario Castellanos. Translation copyright © 1985 by Alberto Manguel.

Contents

Foreword / xiii
by Isabel Allende

Introduction / 1

Foreword

I CONGRATULATE Alberto Manguel on this selection of stories; it demonstrates great sensitivity and understanding. To be born a woman in Latin America (or in any Third World country) is to have a destiny of servitude or, in the best of cases, of second-class citizenship. It requires a very strong spirit, great lucidity, and a good star to overcome the luck of the draw that society has reserved for us. The writers he has chosen have done so. To read them is a fiesta for me.

In this selection of stories I feel interpreted as a Latin American woman. These writers of diverse Latin American countries have expressed our fears and hopes, our delicate ceremonies, our secrets and rebellions, our love and rancor. They are feminine voices trying to interpret the hidden meaning of the sexuality, the power, the ambition, and the injustice of the macho world where they must live. This anthology demonstrates that Latin American women have their own vision of the world and know how to express it in their own personal, irreverent, furious, fantastic, ironic, and poetic language. They tell of the multiple forms of violence they suffer and, in doing so, violate the first rule imposed upon them since birth: the rule of silence. They do not accept it; they do not bow their heads; they do not resign themselves; they are not silent. These stories were written with tears, blood, and kisses.

Isabel Allende

OTHER FIRES

Introduction

LATIN AMERICA IS an imaginary place. From the time when the first Europeans landed on the shores of what they believed to be India, to the time when foreign newspapers, college courses, politicians, anthologies carelessly label as "Latin American" anything that comes from any of the twenty-seven countries that (with the exception of Canada and the United States) occupy the American continent, Latin America has become a monstrously distended Oz populated by gauchos and mariachis, Aztec temples and Caracas skyscrapers, tropical forests and Patagonian plains. In the foreign imagination, an equalizing, all-embracing blanket covers this immense territory, and earnest cultural tourists try hard to find common traits in countries as different as Paraguay and Bolivia, Argentina and Peru. In this sense, the subtitle of *Other Fires* is of course misleading. It seems to imply that the stories in this collection, because they were written by women from several Latin American countries, share a common style, a unified view of the world, an identical history, even the same language. Nothing could be further from either the truth or the editor's intentions.

There have been changes in the stereotype: after years of believing that all Latin American countries look like a set for Carmen Miranda, many now imagine that they all resemble either Gabriel García Márquez's Macondo or El Salvador torn by war. Whatever the stereotype, its uselessness is due less to the fact that even in the case of Colombia or El Salvador these images are incomplete, than to the fact that the stereotype is applied to define a nonexistent entity. Latin America does not exist, and there is no such thing as Latin American literature. There is Argentine literature, Venezuelan literature, Brazilian literature; there is a literature of Chile and a literature of Peru, a literature of Colombia and a literature of Uruguay. Each of these literatures has evolved in its own way and with diverse fortunes. The Chilean Isabel Allende has less in common with the Mexican Juan Rulfo than the German Günther Grass has with the Italian Elsa Morante. Latin America is a tag used by most readers (myself included) out of laziness.

It is true that most Latin American literatures share a predilection for two specific types of fictionalized reality: magic realism and political realism. The former, already found in the writings of the conquistadores who saw the New World in images borrowed from their novels of chivalry, sometimes colors the latter, the baroque and yet precise chronicle of social events. However, both these styles have evolved differently and with varying degrees of success in each individual country and in the work of each individual writer.

Among European and North American readers, an interest in these Latin American literatures began to flourish in the 1960s. First France—urged by Roger Caillois through *La Croix du Sud*, the Latin American series he created for Gallimard—then the United States, Germany, and Italy began to express a discreet interest in a handful of writers from that "remote" part of the world: Borges, García Márquez, Vargas Llosa. And certain books—*Labyrinths*, *A Hundred Years of Solitude*, *The Green House*—entered that exclusive club known as Classic World Literature. But the interest overleapt its object. Outside these few authors very little else was read, and yet this "passion for Latin American literature" became fashionable to the point of silliness: Carlos Fuentes graced the columns of *Playboy*, and Manuel Puig smiled from the pages of *Uomo Vogue*.

In the meantime, quite a number of first-class writers were being translated and ignored: Adolfo Bioy Casares, whose novels *Plan for Escape* and *Asleep in the Sun* (in the impeccable translations of Suzanne Jill Levine) are masterpieces of modern fantastic literature; Ernesto Sábato's monumental *On Heroes and Tombs*; Severo Sarduy, Lezama Lima, Augusto Roa Bastos. . . . The list seems endless.

And yet one fact is striking: among the authors translated, there were hardly any women. A few of the Brazilian writers —Lygia Fagundes Telles, Clarice Lispector—an occasional novel by Beatriz Guido or Elena Garro, a few books by Luisa Valenzuela, and recently a splendid novel by Isabel Allende, *The House of the Spirits*, crept into the publishers' lists. But where were the others? Where was Silvina Ocampo, surely one of the ten best writers writing in Spanish today? Where was Alejandra Pizarnik? Why had no one published in English the works of Amparo Dávila or Armonía Somers or Elena Poniatowska? Why was Marta Lynch, one of the best-selling novelists in the Spanish-speaking world, not translated into English?

This collection does not provide answers to those questions, but it does intend to show something of what is being missed. The writers are all women because it struck the editor as curious that so many of the best untranslated books from Latin American countries had been written by women.

As will become clear in this collection, these writers do not speak with a common, unified voice. Their interests, styles, points of view, are so different that the only justification for their inclusion in the same book is the fact that their excellence has been, up to now, neglected in Europe and North America.

This neglect is even more unjustifiable when set against the fact that, while the literature from Latin American countries has become identified almost exclusively with writers who happen to be male, it owes much to two writers who, separated by three centuries and almost the entire continent, happened to be female. And each, in her own way, expressed an urgent demand for the rights of women.

If we leave aside the remarkable pre-Columbian literature of the Mayas and Aztecs, the first Latin American writer of distinction is a Mexican nun: Sister Juana Inés de la Cruz. Her name in the world was Juana Inés de Asbaje y Ramírez, and she was born in Mexico City in 1648. By the time she was fourteen, her reputation for learning was such that the Viceroy's wife, keen on celebrities and freaks, invited the adolescent to live at the court. An unhappy love affair (as the more romantic historians have it) or perhaps the need for seclusion in order to study led her to enter a Carmelite convent, which she abandoned nine months later. Then in 1669 she joined the Hieronymite order and began writing delicate lyrical poems, satirical verse, and plays in the manner of Calderón de la Barca. Her superiors commanded her to give up her studies "as unbefitting a nun and a woman." In response to this order, she composed an *Answer to Sister Filotea de la Cruz* in which, with grace and intelligence, she defends women's rights to learning. With great wit, she attacks a society dominated by men and a church dominated by the Inquisition, saying that "if she did not write sacred texts, it was because artistic harmony was not within the reach of the Holy Office."

Towards the end of her life, the pressures of the church and lay society became too great, and Sister Juana Inés de la Cruz sold her library of 4,000 books, her musical instruments (she could play with "wonder and ease"), her scientific equipment, and dedicated herself to prayer and charitable works. She died a victim of the plague that ravaged Mexico City in 1695.

Perhaps her best-known poem is (to give it its full title) "Against the Inconsequence of Men's Taste and Strictures, When They Attack Those Qualities in Women of Which They Are Themselves the Cause." The first three quatrains are often quoted:

> You stupid men, who will defame
> all womankind, and baselessly,
> blind to the fact that you might be
> the cause of just that which you blame;
>
> if with unequalled ardour you
> pay constant court to their disdain,
> how have them virtuous remain
> and still incite them sinful too?
>
> You fight till their resistance sways,
> and later solemnly declare
> that what your diligence worked there
> was due to lightness of their ways.

Translated by Richard Outram

Three centuries later, and in Argentina, another woman accused men of many of the same faults, but on a vaster, social and political, scale. Born into a rich and aristocratic family, Victoria Ocampo used her social advantages to open the doors of Argentina to the rest of the world. She did this through her magazine, Sur, which introduced Argentine readers to contemporary world literature. At the same time, Victoria Ocampo herself became a symbol of Argentine culture. Virginia Woolf, Aldous Huxley, Waldo Frank, André Malraux, Graham Greene, Igor Stravinsky, Rabindranath Tagore, are just a few of the personalities she brought to Argentina. She was the first to publish in Spanish the works of William Faulkner, Virginia Woolf, Yukio Mishima,

Thomas Merton. She campaigned for Borges even before Borges had achieved the fullness of his craft and obtained for him the post of Director of the National Library after the Peronist government had demoted him to chicken inspector at one of the municipal markets.

In 1936 Victoria Ocampo founded the Women's Union. Doris Meyer, in her excellent biography, quotes from one of the speeches she delivered that year:

> Until the present, we have heard principally from male witnesses concerning women, witnesses that a court of law would not allow since they would be considered suspect, male witnesses whose testimony is biased. The woman herself has scarcely uttered a word. And it is up to the woman not only to discover this unexplored continent she represents, but also to talk in turn about men in her own capacity as suspect witness.

> If she manages to do this, world literature will be enriched beyond calculation (and I don't doubt that she will).

> I know by my own experience how unprepared the present-day woman is, particularly the South American woman, to achieve this victory. She has neither the necessary training, the freedom or the tradition. And I wonder what can be accomplished by genius alone without these three things; can it produce something of value? The miracle of a work of art is produced only when it has been silently prepared for many years.

> I believe that our generation and the following one, and even the one about to be born, are destined not to achieve this miracle but to prepare for it and make it imminent. I believe our work will be painful and unrecognized. I believe that we must resign ourselves to it with humility, but also with profound faith in its greatness and its fecundity.

In another essay also written in 1936, Victoria Ocampo concludes: "It is incredible, and I speak now without irony, that millions of human beings have not yet understood that current demands made by women are simply limited to requiring that a man stop thinking of a woman as a colony for him to exploit and that she become instead 'the country in which he lives.' "

When Roger Caillois discovered Borges, in his enthusiasm he spoke of "a fire burning on the other side of the Atlantic," much like the fires the Spanish explorers had seen burning on the coast of Patagonia and on what was to be known as Tierra del Fuego (Land of Fire). Alejandra Pizarnik answered Caillois's remark in a poem:

> We also have built durable fires
> But mine
> As high as yours and as changing
> Hides behind the hands upon your eyes.
> Their reflection burns.
> (The dark reflections
> Of other, all-consuming flames.)

This collection intends to show a few of these "other fires," but all selections are arbitrary, all choices mysterious. The reasons for an anthology comes afterwards, after the irrational gods have dictated our likes and dislikes. In the end, an anthology reflects less the theme it pretends to anthologize than the editor's voice, taste, memory. That sharing of a personal affection is this book's only true justification.

Alberto Manguel
Toronto 1985

The Fall

———

ARMONÍA SOMERS

IN URUGUAY, Armonía Somers's fiction (her real name is Armonía Etchepare de Henestrosa) is not widely read; her reputation is that of a teacher and author of teaching manuals. Her complete stories were published in the 1960s by Angel Rama, the Uruguayan editor and critic who did so much to promote Latin American literature in Latin America itself, but they never sold well. And yet her fiction is among the most intricately crafted in Spanish, blending the language of the sixteenth-century Spanish poets with a vividly contemporary imagination. Angel Rama considered Armonía Somers the inheritor of the early surrealists and reminded the reader that the Count of Lautréamont (the great French surrealist whose landscapes seem to invade Somers's stories) was, like the author of "The Fall," also born in Montevideo.

"STILL RAINING. Damn you, Holy Virgin, damn you. Why, why is it still raining?" Too dark a thought for his black voice, for the soft saliva-tasting humble black sounds. That's why he had only imagined the words. He could never allow them to escape, into the air. And even as a thought they were something wicked, something bad for his white negro conscience. He had always prayed, spoken, differently; like a lover:

"Help me, my Lady, white Rose of the rose-bush. Help this poor nigger who killed the big brute of a white man, who did just that, today. My only Rose, please help him, my Heart of sweet almond, bring this nigger a little good luck, my bright garden Rose."

But not tonight. It was cold and it was raining. His bones were drenched to the point where the cold hurt the bone. He had lost one of his shoes walking in the mud, and his toes had come out through the other one. Every time a sharp stone lay in his path, the bare toes would hit against it violently, against that stone and not another, never against a smooth, round stone. And the blow on the toes was hardly painful compared to the savage pain that soared up the branches of his body and then fell back again, back to his toes, gripping onto them, hard, painfully hard. It was at times like these that he felt unable to understand his white, white Rose. How could She do this to him? Because the sweet Lady should have warned him that the stone was there, in his way. She should also have made it stop raining so hard, so hard and cold.

The black man kept his hands stuffed into his pockets, his hat pulled down to his shoulders, the old suit buttoned up as far as the few buttons allowed. But the suit was no longer a suit; it was a rag, sodden, shining, as slippery as spit. The body was shaped under the cloth, showing perfect, harmonious black curves. And also—he kept saying to himself—She should have made night fall faster. He had needed night so much throughout the day. There was not a single hole left out there to hide this nigger's fear, in the blazing light. And only now had the white Rose sent him the gift of night.

The black man's tread was slow, persistent. Like the rain, it neither quickened nor slackened its pace. At times he and the rain seemed to know each other too well to be enemies, fighting one another, but not wounding their opponents. Also, the rain made music.

He arrived at last. How he had longed for this place! A short distance from paradise his eyes would not have shone as bright. Yes: the ramshackle house stood there alone, in the night. He had never been inside, but he had heard of it. More than once he had been told about this "safe place," but that was all.

"My rose-white Lady!"

This time he called Her with a full voice. A bolt of lightning cut out his figure, bony and long and black, against the night. Then a blast in the sky, a rough, painful blow, sharp like the one against his toes. He touched his thighs through the ripped lining of his pockets. No, he hadn't vanished into the ground. He felt suddenly happy, humbly and tenderly happy to be still alive. And the bolt had allowed him to see the house clearly. He could have sworn he had seen it move during the blast. But the house had steadied itself, like a woman recovering from a fainting spell. All around the house were ruins, where they had swept away those shacks by the river. Prostitution had made its nest there some time ago, but now all that was left was rubble, these walls left standing because of some unexplained whim. He saw it all, admiring the beautiful hovel, its lost loneliness, its locked-in silence. Now he not only saw it; he could almost touch it if he wanted to. But then, just like someone who is about to reach what he most wants, the black man felt he did not dare. He had walked so long, suffered so much to get here, that it all now seemed unreal, inviolate. The house. On both sides were bits of wall, desolate heaps of rubbish, piles of mud. With each flash of lightning the house appeared again. Everywhere he could see vertical cracks. Also a low door, and two windows, one at the front, one at the side.

The black man, with almost sacrilegious terror, knocked on the door. His fingers hurt, stiff, petrified by the cold. The rain kept falling. He knocked a second time; still no one came to open. He wanted to seek cover, but the house had no eaves, nothing hospitable on the outside. It had been different, walking under the rain. It had seemed different to brave the drifting heavens, out there. The real rain was not like this. The real rain was the one borne by the toes, the stones, all anchored things. It was only then that one could say it rained within, that the liquid world weighed down, destroyed, dissolved. For the third time he knocked with cold, stone fingers, black onyx fingers with tender yellow rose-tips. The fourth time he used his fist. And here the black man made a mistake; he thought they had come to open because he had knocked louder.

The fourth time was the number of the code established by the house. A man appeared carrying a shaded lamp.

"Master, master, let this poor nigger in."

"Go on, damn you, get in!"

He closed the door behind him and lifted the lamp, black with soot, as high as he could. The negro was tall, as if on stilts. And the other man, damn it, was short. He could see his face. It was white, wrinkled vertically, like plaster scratched with nails. From the corner of his lips to the edge of his left eyebrow ran a savage scar of unmistakable origin. The scar followed the line of the lips, the thin lips, making the whole mouth look enormous and lopsided, all the way up to the eyebrow. The eyes were piercing and small, with no lashes, and the nose was Roman. The black man snapped out of the gaze and said in a honeyed voice:

"How much, master?"

"Two prices, you choose. Quickly, nigger. Ten for the camp bed, two for the floor," came the reply, harsh, while the man shielded the lamp with his hand.

That was it. Ten cents and two. The bed, the luxury, the solitary bed lay almost always empty.

The black man looked at the floor. Full. From the bodies rose a unified snore, heaving like sounds from a midnight swamp.

"I'll take the two cents one, master," he said humbly, bending over.

The man with the scar lifted his lamp once more, and wound his way back among the bodies. The black man followed him along the twisting path, like a dog. For the time being, the white man did not care whether the visitor had money with him or not. He would find out once the negro fell asleep, even though the search was usually fruitless. Only someone who had been tricked would arrive here with money. The house was a tramp's establishment, the last refuge on a doorless night. He could not remember whether he had ever rented out the bed. Now it had become the owner's own.

"There you are. Lie down," he said at last, stopping, his voice as sharp and cold as the cut on his face. "Naked or as you are. You're lucky, you'll be between these two heaps. But if another one arrives you'll have to make room for him. This ditch is large enough for two, or three, or twenty."

The black man looked down from his height. In the broken floor, no one knew why, was a kind of valley, soft and warm like the space between two bodies.

He was about to take his clothes off. He was about to become part of the sea of heaving backs, stomachs, snores, smells, ghoulish dreams, sighs, moans. It was then, after the white man had blown out the light next to the single bed, that he discovered the image of the white Rose Herself, with a small flickering flame burning in oil, high upon a shelf on the wall he was supposed to be facing.

"Master, master!"

"Will you shut up?"

"Tell me," he asked, ignoring the order, "Do you believe in the white Lady?"

The raw laugh of the scarred man on the bed cut through the air.

"Me? Believe? You ignorant nigger! I've got Her there just in case She's in charge, eh? That way She can see to it that the roof doesn't fall down on me."

He was about to laugh again, that laugh so like his face, but he couldn't finish it. A blast of thunder that seemed to come from underneath the earth shook the house. It was different in here, thought the black man. It drummed inside his guts, deep inside him. Then the rain, the wind, whipped up again. The side window was being furiously beaten; it seemed to shake in an epileptic fit.

Above the sounds, the black man's strong smell took over. It seemed to drown them, the sounds, the other smells, as if fighting against them all.

Sleep. But how? If he kept his clothes on, it would be like sleeping in water. If he took them off, the skin on his bones would feel drenched. He chose the skin, thinking that it would somehow lend warmth to the icy puddles. And he let himself fall into the ditch, stark naked. The light of the Virgin's lamp began to turn softer, clearer, as if the shadows had fed the oil, black as the black man's skin. From the Virgin's wall to the wall opposite someone had hung a dirty gauze, flapping obsessively, swinging in the seeping wind. It was a sample of the ancient weaving that had grown within the house. Every time the wind grew stronger, the gauze's dance became more dazzling, maddening. The black man covered his ears and thought, "If I were deaf I still wouldn't be free of the wind. I'd see it, Holy Mother, in that spider's web, I'd see it, and I'd die from seeing it."

He began to shiver. He touched his forehead; it seemed on fire. At times his whole body seemed to burn. Then it would fall into ice, shaking and sweating. He wanted to wrap himself up in something, but what? No use. He'd have to brave it naked, powerless, in the ditch. How was he to stand the shivering, the sweating, the helplessness, the cold? No way of knowing. And the pain in his back was stabbing him. He tried to close his eyes, to sleep. Perhaps in sleep he'd forget it all. There was much to forget, not only his body. What he had done that day with these, his hands, now part of the pain in his flesh. . . .

But first he tried looking at the Lady. There She stood, tender, soft, white, watching over the sleepers. The man had a dark thought. How could She be there, among so many lost souls, in the midst of that dirty human mass from which a strong stench arose, a filthiness of bodies and rags, fetid breath, crimes, vices, bad dreams? He looked at the strong mixture of men, sins and lice, spread out on the floor, snoring, while She, on Her shelf, kept on quietly shining.

And he? He thought about himself, saw his own nakedness. He was the worst of the lot. The others at least didn't show their flesh to the Virgin as he did, their uncovered shame. He should hide that, not offend the Immaculate Eyes, cover it somehow. He tried. But he couldn't bring himself to do it. Cold, heat, shivers, a stab in the back, dead will, longing for sleep. He couldn't, perhaps he would never be able to, ever again. He'd lie forever in this ditch, unable to cry out that he was dying, unable to pray to the Good Lady, beg Her forgiveness for his coal-black nakedness, his jutting bones, his overpowering odour, and worse, for what his hands had done.

It was then that it happened. The white Rose began to climb down from Her shelf, very slowly. Up there She had seemed to him as small as a doll—small, compact, shapeless. But as She descended She grew—carnal, sweet, alive. The black man felt he was dying. His fear and his surprise were larger than himself, outgrew him. He tried to touch his own body, make sure of his presence, simply to believe in something. But he couldn't. Outside his pain and shivering, he felt nothing. Everything seemed impossible, faraway, like another world lost in another time. Except for this: the approaching Woman.

The white Rose wouldn't stop. Her descent was something decisive, like running water, like rising light. But the most terrible thing about it was the direction of Her movement. Could one doubt that She was coming towards him, towards *him*, the most naked and filthy of men? Now She was almost by his side. He could see Her dainty shoes of golden glazed earthenware, the rim of Her pale blue cloak.

The black man tried to get up. Useless. His terror, his trembling, his shame, had nailed him with his back to the ground. Then he heard the voice, the sweetest honey life can offer:

"Tristan. . . ."

Yes, he remembered being called that in a faraway time on the other side of that door. It was therefore true; the Lady had come down, Her earthenware feet were real, the trimming of Her cloak was true. He would have to answer or die. He would have to speak, acknowledge the arriving Flower. He tried to swallow. Thick, bitter, insufficient spit. But it helped, a little.

"You, white rose-bush Rose. . . ."

"Yes, Tristan. Can you move?"

"No, my Lady. I don't know why. Everything stays up here, in the thoughts, and won't go down to my body. I can't believe it's You, my clear Pearl, I can't believe it."

"It is true, Tristan. Don't doubt Me."

Then, incredibly, the Virgin knelt by his side. It had always been otherwise; now the Virgin humbled Herself before a black man.

"Holy Mother of God, don't do that! No, my solitary Rose on the bush, don't do that!"

"Yes, Tristan, and not only kneel, which hurts Me terribly. Other things I'll do tonight that I never dared do. And you will help Me."

"Help You, Water Lily? With these hands that will do nothing now, but that today. . . . Oh, I can't tell You, my Lady, what they've done! Rose of amber, forgive this good nigger who turned bad on this black day!"

"Give Me that hand you killed with, Tristan."

"How do You know it was a nigger who killed that man, my Lady?"

"Don't talk like an unbeliever, Tristan. Give Me your hand."

"I can't lift it. . . ."

"Then I will come to the hand," She said with a voice that seemed to grow less vague, more alive.

And now a new impossibility occurred in that descent. The Virgin pressed Her waxen lips against the hard, bony hand of the black man, and kissed it.

"Holy Mother of God, I can't resist it!"

"Yes, Tristan. I've kissed the hand you killed with. And I will tell you why. It was I who told you the words you heard inside you: *Don't stop, press harder, finish with him now, don't hesitate!*"

"You, Mother of the Child!"

"Yes, Tristan, and you have said the word. They killed my Child. They would kill Him again, were He to return. I won't go on. I want no more pearls, prayers, tears, perfume, songs. Someone had to be the first to pay; you helped Me. I've waited peacefully, but now I've understood that I must begin. My Child, my poor and sweet Child, sacrificed in vain! How

I cried, how I soaked in tears His torn and mangled body! Tristan, you don't know the worst."

"What, Little Mother?"

"I could never cry after that day for His loss. Since I was made marble, wax, sculpted wood, gold, ivory, I've had no tears. I had to carry on living this way, with a lie of stupid smiles painted on My face. Tristan, I was not what they have painted. I was different, certainly less beautiful. And I have come to tell you something."

"Yes, my Lady. Tell this nigger."

"Tristan, you will be frightened by what I am about to do."

"I am dying of fright, my Lily, but I am still alive."

"Tristan," said the Virgin, Her voice more sure, almost more human. "I will lie by your side. Didn't the white man say there was room for two here in the ditch?"

"No, no, Little Mother! My tongue is fainting, I can hardly ask You any longer not to do it!"

"Tristan, do you know what you are doing? You are praying, ever since you saw Me. No one has ever prayed like this to Me before. . . ."

"I'll sing You a sweeter tune, I'll sing and cry like the reeds, but please, please don't lie by the side of this bad nigger!"

"Yes, Tristan, I am doing it. Watch Me do it."

And the black man saw how the figure lay down by his side with a rustle of silk and necklaces, with Her smell of time and virginity mingled in Her hair.

"And now comes the most important part, Tristan. You must take these clothes off Me. Start with the shoes. They are instruments of torture, as if made of rigid iron, destroying My feet on which I must stand throughout the centuries. Take them off, Tristan, please. I can bear them no longer."

"Yes, I will free Your feet in pain with these sinner's hands. That, yes, clear Lady."

"Oh, Tristan, the relief! But you haven't finished, Tristan.

See how ridiculous they look, My feet. They are made of wax: feel them, made of wax."

"Yes, my Lady of the waxen feet, they are of wax."

"But now you will learn something important, Tristan. Inside the waxen feet I have got feet of flesh and blood."

"Holy Mother, You are killing me!"

"Yes, I am flesh and blood under the wax."

"No, no, Little Mother. Go back on the shelf. This nigger doesn't want the Holy Mother of flesh to lie by his side in the dark. Go back, sweet Rose, go back to Your place of roses!"

"No, Tristan, I'm not going back. When a Virgin has left her site She can never go back to it. I want you to melt My wax. I cannot be the Immaculate; I am the true Mother of the Child they killed. I need to walk, hate, cry on this earth. I need to be of flesh, not cold and lifeless wax."

"And how can I, sweet Lady, melt the wax?"

"Touch me, Tristan, fondle Me. A moment ago your hands would not answer. Since I kissed them they are moving. You understand what your touch will do. Start now. Touch My waxen feet, you will see how the cast melts."

"Yes, my wonderful Pearl, that, yes. Your feet must be set free, in spite of stones. And I will touch them, there. And I can feel it happening, Little Mother. Look, look how the wax melts in my fingers. . . ."

"And now touch my real feet, Tristan."

"They are two live gardenias, two feet made of flowers. . . ."

"But that is not enough. Go on and free My legs."

"The Rose's legs? No, I can't, I can't go on melting. That frightens me. This nigger is very frightened."

"On, Tristan, on."

"I can feel the knee, my captive Lady. And that is all. Here I stop this savage deed, this nigger deed. . . . I swear I'll stop. Cut off my hands, sweet Mother of the Blond Child, cut them off. And make this nigger forget he ever had these hands, forget he touched the Holy Flower's stem. Cut them off, with a knife sharpened in blood."

A furious blast thundered through the night. The windows beat against their frames, shaking. The house quivered like a ship.

"Have you heard, have you seen how things are tonight? If you don't continue melting, everything will be over for Me before morning. Go on, hurry, finish melting My thighs. I need My whole legs to be Mine once again."

"Yes, soft thighs, terror of this lost nigger. Here they are, warm and silky, like lizards under a winter's sun. But no more, Little Virgin. See how I cry. These tears are my blood aching inside this nigger."

"Have you heard, Tristan, and seen? The house is shaking once more. Don't be afraid of My thighs. Go on, go on melting."

"But we are near the golden bud, my Lady. The locked garden. I can't, I shouldn't!"

"Touch it, Tristan, touch that, especially that. When the wax there melts you need go no further. Then the wax on My breasts, on My back, on My belly, will melt on their own. Do it, Tristan. I want you to do it."

"No, my Lady. Not the golden bud. That I can't."

"It will still be the same, Tristan. Do you think it will change because you've touched it?"

"But it is not only touching it. It is that one can want it so much, with one's blood, with this crazy nigger blood. Have pity, my Lady. This nigger doesn't want to lose himself forever. With tears I beg You to leave him."

"Do it. Look Me in the eyes and do it."

Then the black man lifted his eyes up to the Virgin and saw two forget-me-nots sparkling with celestial fire, like the breath of a chimera. He could no longer disobey. He felt She would consume him.

"I knew it, I knew it. Why did I do it? Why did I touch it? Now I want to enter, now I want to sink into the dampness of that garden. Now this poor nigger can stand it no longer. Look, forbidden Lady, how this nigger's life is trembling, how his mad blood is rising to choke him. I knew I should not have touched it. Let me enter that tight ring, my captive Lady, and then kill this nigger trapped in his own disgrace."

"Tristan, you won't, you won't. You have achieved something greater. Do you know what you've done?"

"Yes, sweet Palm Tree of this nigger's dreams. Yes, I know the terrible thing I've done."

"No, you don't know all of it. You have melted a Virgin. What you now want is unimportant. It is enough for a man to know how to melt a Virgin. That is a man's true glory."

"That's too hard for this poor nigger's head. That's for the clear head of One Who comes from Heaven."

"Tristan: another thing you don't know. Tristan: you're dying."

The black man sank his head between the Woman's breasts, among the smell of blossoming flowers.

"I had forgotten, Little Mother!" he suddenly cried out, as if possessed. "It has come back to me, here, in Your Childless milk! They want to lynch me! I have touched one of their creatures! Let me go, sweet Lady, let me get away! Let me escape! Let me go, Little Mother, let me go!"

"Not so loud, Tristan, the others on the floor will wake up," said the Woman softly, as in a lullaby. "Keep quiet. Nothing can touch you now. Can you hear? The wind. This house hasn't fallen because I am here. But something worse could happen to it, even with Me under its roof. Be sure."

"What? What could that be?"

"I'll tell you. They have hunted all day. Only this place remains; they left it till the last, as usual. In a few seconds they'll be here. They will come because you killed that brute. And they won't care if you're dying naked in this hole. They will trample the others, they will fall on you. They will drag you outside by an arm or a leg."

"Little Mother, don't let them!"

"No, I won't let them. How could I? You are the one who helped Me come out of My wax. I won't forget you."

"How will You stop them from catching me alive?"

"I only have to leave by that window. Now I have feet that move; you gave them to Me," She said in a secret whisper. "They will knock. You know how many times they must knock. At the fourth knock the white man will leave his bed. They will come to get you. But I won't be there. If you were not dying I'd take you with Me, We'd jump through the window together. But in these cases Our Father can do more than I can. You cannot escape your death. All I can do is stop them catching you alive."

"And then, Holy Mother?" said the black man, kneeling up in spite of his weakness.

"You know, Tristan, what will happen without Me in this house."

"Listen. . . . They're knocking. That's the first time. . . ."

"Tristan, upon the second knock We will hold each other tightly," the Woman whispered, also rising to Her knees.

The man with the scar heard the knocking and stood up. He lit the lamp.

"Now, Tristan."

The black man held the Virgin tight. He sniffed Her real hair, real woman's hair, then pressed his face against Her human cheek.

The third knock on the door. The scarred man moved among the sleepers on the floor. This was not the usual kind of knocking, the kind he recognized. This was a knocking with a full stomach, with a gun in the hand.

At that very moment the Woman opened the side window. Thin and light like a half-moon, She needed barely the slightest gap to escape. A sad, languid wind carried her away into the night.

"Mother, Mother, don't leave me! That was the fourth knock! I remember what their death is like! Any death, except theirs!"

"Shut up, you stupid nigger!" said the white man. "I bet it's because of you they're here. You swine! I thought as much!"

Then it happened. They entered like flung stones, full of eyes. They went straight towards the black man, holding their lamps ahead of them, treading, kicking the others like rotten fruit. An infernal wind followed them in. The house began to shake again, as it had done several times that night. But the Virgin was no longer in the house. There was a crack, like a skeleton snapping. Then, a world falling apart—the rumble that can be heard before something crumbles down, before a fall.

It happened. Suddenly. Over everyone, over the dead man and over the ones who had come to drag him out.

Of course the rain had stopped. The wind seemed freer, harsher and more naked, licking up the dust, the dust of annihilation.

Translated by Alberto Manguel

Metonymy, or
The Husband's Revenge

RACHEL DE QUEIROZ

FOUR NOVELS, which she wrote between the ages of nineteen and twenty-eight, established Rachel de Queiroz's reputation as one of Brazil's best writers, intent on defying the traditionally submissive role that women held in Brazilian literature. It is interesting that she chose the melodramatic plots of many turn-of-the-century novels—tales of disgruntled heroines who must purge the sin of breaking the rules of society —and turned these plots against themselves. Her heroines triumph in their revolt, not in their punishment; it is the laws of society, not the women (says de Queiroz), which are to blame. Since the 1930s, when her four novels were published, de Queiroz has worked mainly as a critic and translator. The exceptions have been a few plays, and one other novel, Brandão between His Love and the Sea, *written in collaboration with three other distinguished Brazilian novelists: Jorge Amado, Lins do Rêgo, and Graciliano Ramos.*

METONYMY. I LEARNED the word in 1930 and shall never forget it. I had just published my first novel. A literary critic had scolded me because my hero went out into the night "chest unbuttoned."

"What deplorable nonsense!" wrote this eminently sensible gentleman. "Why does she not say what she means? Obviously, it was his shirt that was unbuttoned, not his chest."

I accepted his rebuke with humility, indeed with shame. But my illustrious Latin professor, Dr. Matos Peixoto, came to my rescue. He said that what I had written was perfectly correct; that I had used a respectable figure of speech known as metonymy; and that this figure consisted in the use of one word for another word associated with it—for example, a word representing a cause instead of the effect, or representing the container when the content is intended. The classic instance, he told me, is "the sparkling cup"; in reality, not the cup but the wine in it is sparkling.

The professor and I wrote a letter, which was published in the newspaper where the review had appeared. It put my unjust critic in his place. I hope he learned a lesson. I know I did. Ever since, I have been using metonymy—my only bond with classical rhetoric.

Moreover, I have devoted some thought to it, and I have concluded that metonymy may be more than a figure of speech. There is, I believe, such a thing as practical or applied metonymy. Let me give a crude example, drawn from my own experience. A certain lady of my acquaintance suddenly moved out of the boardinghouse where she had been living for years and became a mortal enemy of the woman who owned it. I asked her why. We both knew that the woman was a kindly soul; she had given my friend injections when she needed them, had often loaned her a hot water bottle, and had always waited on her when she had her little heart attacks. My friend replied:

"It's the telephone in the hall. I hate her for it. Half the time when I answered it, the call was a hoax or joke of some sort."

"But the owner of the boardinghouse didn't perpetrate these hoaxes. She wasn't responsible for them."

"No. But whose telephone was it?"

I know another case of applied metonymy, a more disastrous one for it involved a crime. It happened in a city of the interior, which I shall not name for fear that someone may recognize the parties and revive the scandal. I shall narrate the crime but conceal the criminal.

Well, in this city of the interior there lived a man. He was not old but he was spent, which is worse than being old. In his youth he had suffered from beriberi. His legs were weak, his chest was tired and asthmatic, his skin was yellowish, and his eyes were rheumy. He was, however, a man of property; he owned the house in which he lived and the one next to it, in which he had set up a grocery store. Therefore, although so unattractive personally, he was able to find himself a wife. In all justice to him, he did not tempt fate by marrying a beauty. Instead, he married a poor, emaciated girl who worked in a men's clothing factory. By her face one would have thought that she had consumption. So our friend felt safe. He did not foresee the effects of good nutrition and a healthful life on a woman's appearance. The girl no longer spent eight hours a day at a sewing table. She was the mistress of her house. She ate well: fresh meat, cucumber salad, pork fat with beans and manioc mush, all kinds of sweets, and oranges, which her husband bought by the gross for his customers. The effects were like magic. Her body filled out, especially in the best places. She even seemed to grow taller. And her face—what a change! I may have forgotten to mention that her features, in themselves, were good to begin with. Moreover, money enabled her to embellish her natural advantages with art; she began to wear make-up, to wave her hair, and to dress well.

Lovely, attractive, she now found her sickly, prematurely old husband a burden and a bore. Each evening, as soon as the store was closed, he dined, mostly on milk (he could not stomach meat), took his newspaper, and rested on his chaise longue until time to go to bed. He did not care for movies or for soccer or for radio. He did not even show much interest in love. Just a sort of tepid, tasteless cohabitation.

And then Fate intervened: it produced a sergeant.

Granted, it was unjust for a young wife, after being reconditioned at her husband's expense, to employ her charms against the aforesaid husband. Unjust; but, then, this world thrives on injustice, doesn't it? The sergeant—I shall not say whether he was in the Army, the Air Force, the Marines, or the Fusiliers, for I still mean to conceal the identities of the parties—the sergeant was muscular, young, ingratiating, with a manly, commanding voice and a healthy spring in his walk. He looked gloriously martial in his high-buttoned uniform.

One day, when the lady was in charge of the counter (while her husband lunched), the sergeant came in. Exactly what happened and what did not happen, is hard to say. It seems that the sergeant asked for a pack of cigarettes. Then he wanted a little vermouth. Finally he asked permission to listen to the sports broadcast on the radio next to the counter. Maybe it was just an excuse to remain there awhile. In any case, the girl said it would be all right. It is hard to refuse a favour to a sergeant, especially a sergeant like this one. It appears that the sergeant asked nothing more that day. At most, he and the girl exchanged expressive glances and a few agreeable words, murmured so softly that the customers, always alert for something to gossip about, could not hear them.

Three times more the husband lunched while his wife chat-

ted with the sergeant in the store. The flirtation progressed.
Then the husband fell ill with a grippe, and the two others
went far beyond flirtation. How and where they met, no one
was able to discover. The important thing is that they were
lovers and that they loved with a forbidden love, like Tristan
and Isolde or Paolo and Francesca.

Then Fate, which does not like illicit love and generally
punishes those who engage in it, transferred the sergeant to
another part of the country.

It is said that only those who love can really know the pain
of separation. The girl cried so much that her eyes grew red
and swollen. She lost her appetite. Beneath her rouge could
be seen the consumptive complexion of earlier times. And
these symptoms aroused her husband's suspicion, although,
curiously, he had never suspected anything when the love
affair was flourishing and everything was wine and roses.

He began to observe her carefully. He scrutinized her in
her periods of silence. He listened to her sighs and to the
things she murmured in her sleep. He snooped around and
found a postcard and a book, both with a man's name in the
same handwriting. He found the insignia of the sergeant's
regiment and concluded that the object of his wife's mur-
murs, sighs, and silences was not only a man but a soldier.
Finally he made the supreme discovery: that they had indeed
betrayed him. For he discovered the love letters, bearing air-
mail stamps, a distant postmark, and the sergeant's name.
They left no reasonable doubt.

For five months the poor fellow twisted the poisoned dag-
ger of jealousy inside his own thin, sickly chest. Like a boy
who discovers a bird's nest and, hiding nearby, watches the
eggs increasing in number every day, so the husband, using a
duplicate key to the wood chest where his wife put her valu-
ables, watched the increase in the number of letters con-

cealed there. He had given her the chest during their honeymoon, saying, "Keep your secrets here." And the ungrateful girl had obeyed him.

Every day at the fateful hour of lunch, she replaced her husband at the counter. But he was not interested in eating. He ran to her room, pulled out a drawer in her bureau, removed the chest from under a lot of panties, slips, and such, took the little key out of his pocket, opened the chest, and anxiously read the new letter. If there was no new letter, he reread the one dated August 21st; it was so full of realism that it sounded like dialogue from a French movie. Then he put everything away and hurried to the kitchen, where he swallowed a few spoonfuls of broth and gnawed at a piece of bread. It was almost impossible to swallow with the passion of those two thieves sticking in his throat.

When the poor man's heart had become utterly saturated with jealousy and hatred, he took a revolver and a box of bullets from the counter drawer; they had been left, years before, by a customer as security for a debt which had never been paid. He loaded the revolver.

One bright morning at exactly ten o'clock, when the store was full of customers, he excused himself and went through the doorway that connected the store with his home. In a few seconds the customers heard the noise of a row, a woman's scream, and three shots. On the sidewalk in front of the shopkeeper's house they saw his wife on her knees, still screaming, and him, with the revolver in his trembling hand, trying to raise her. The front door of the house was open. Through it, they saw a man's legs, wearing khaki trousers and boots. He was lying face down, with his head and torso in the parlor, not visible from the street.

The husband was the first to speak. Raising his eyes from his wife, he looked at the terror-stricken people and spotted among them his favourite customer. He took a few steps, stood in the doorway, and said:

"You may call the police."

At the police station he explained that he was a deceived husband. The police chief remarked:

"Isn't this a little unusual? Ordinarily you kill your wives. They're weaker than their lovers."

The man was deeply offended.

"No," he protested. "I would be utterly incapable of killing my wife. She is all that I have in the world. She is refined, pretty, and hard-working. She helps me in the store, she understands bookkeeping, she writes the letters to the wholesalers. She is the only person who knows how to prepare my food. Why should I want to kill my wife?"

"I see," said the chief of police. "So you killed her lover."

The man shook his head.

"Wrong again. The sergeant—her lover—was transferred to a place far from here. I discovered the affair only after he had gone. By reading his letters. They tell the whole story. I know one of them by heart, the worst of them. . . ."

The police chief did not understand. He said nothing and waited for the husband to continue, which he presently did:

"Those letters! If they were alive, I would kill them, one by one. They were shameful to read—almost like a book. I thought of taking an airplane trip. I thought of killing some other sergeant here, so that they would all learn a lesson not to fool around with another man's wife. But I was afraid of the rest of the regiment; you know how these military men stick together. Still, I had to do something. Otherwise I would have gone crazy. I couldn't get those letters out of my head. Even on days when none arrived I felt terrible, worse than my wife. I had to put an end to it, didn't I? So today, at last, I did it. I waited till the regular time and, when I saw the wretch appear on the other side of the street, I went into the house, hid behind a door, and lay there waiting for him."

"The lover?" asked the police chief stupidly.

"No, of course not. I told you I didn't kill her lover. It was those letters. The sergeant sent them—but *he* delivered them. Almost every day, there he was at the door, smiling, with the vile envelope in his hand. I pointed the revolver and fired three times. He didn't say a word; he just fell. No, chief, it wasn't her lover. It was the mailman."

Translated by William L. Grossman

Latin Lover

MARTA LYNCH

MARTA LYNCH'S FIRST novel, La alfombra roja (The Red Carpet), *was the result of her political experience when, as a young woman, she followed the campaign of Arturo Frondizi who became president of Argentina in 1958. The Red Carpet is a brilliant study of the ascent to power, told in several voices, each a character in the political game. The world of politics is always present in Marta Lynch's work. Her most important novel,* La Señora Ordoñez, *is the portrait of a woman looking back from her late middle-age at the history of Argentina: the heroine and the historical events mirror each other, illuminating their mutual secrets. One of her books,* El cruce del rio (The Crossing of the River), *an episode of the guerrilla movement told by a dead* guerrillero *and his mother, was considered too dangerous by the military government and was therefore seized and burned. Marta Lynch's stories depict more intimate themes, the falling in and out of love, the everyday anguishes of everyday characters or, as in "Latin Lover," a tiny moment of victory.*

During the sixties, I had the good fortune of visiting her almost every Sunday for several years and saw her discover—and then share her discovery with us—Hemingway, Turgenev, Katherine Mansfield, Günther Grass. She wanted to write about the society she knew much as these writers had written about theirs. In many cases she succeeded, and her best novels are vigorous social chronicles. Marta Lynch committed suicide in October of 1985.

AT FIRST I THOUGHT he was joking, but no. He simply took it for granted once he had looked round the flat and given me the keys. Standing there among the nylon-covered armchairs and the plastic flowers he made a slight grimace: "It's camp," he informed me. He could just as well have said "crass" or "tacky" as in that bad poem about his congenital aloofness. But he said "camp" and I cringed.

So there: the nylon, the flowers, the narrow bed—it would all be home to me. Light poured in through a high window barely covered by a three-coloured gauze which matched the nylon and the oppressive ashtray (in the shape of a toilet— supposedly the naughty touch—blue, made of china). When he came back from inspecting the kitchen I had hidden it underneath the cushions, but he picked up the cushions and discovered it. He always finds out everything. The Joie de Vivre beauty cream about which he questions me with an amused look. Or a more or less secret letter. Or the bags under my eyes on certain days. Everything. "Put it away, for once we agree." But he also added: "Not bad," and I found myself settled in. From then onwards our life would be a dining-room—a camp dining-room—a bathroom, a kitchen, a small terrace. It would be difficult to see the street from any of the windows: they were all too high, above my line of vision. Except the bedroom window. From there I could see the neighbouring balconies and a noisy road behind the building. He was deciding just how to settle my life in these three camp rooms with all the good will he puts into the things that demand little effort and don't distract him from his purpose.

His brown eyes had a noncommittal look: neither cold nor disheartening. Just eyes. I had loved those eyes with a fury that expressed itself in every gesture. Many times I thought I overwhelmed him, but no. He seemed to accept being adored. I mustn't be unfair: he also adored me, even if it was only from time to time. Nobody expects a man and a woman to reach the same corner at the same time. Maybe, when we decided on the flat, I *did* expect it: but only faintly, like someone complaining, yet knowing she's alone, trapped, in the dark, inside a broken elevator. The alarm goes off and all that comes with it . . . but still one feels sick with anxiety, certain of the danger. I told him I'd be afraid at night, and the words drifted through the room and hung from a pair of fake bronze chandeliers that lit the table.

And I began to live. I could have said it was difficult, but no. That's what's so maddening about it: it isn't even difficult. You could spend your life in a place like this, growing old. This sort of love is a vicious circle that forces one to stay outside. Maybe it was from him that I learned about being an outsider.

I never met a man who looked so much like a travelling salesman; I always felt tempted to hand him his suitcase, but no. To tell the truth, his life was so carefully scheduled I could follow him in my mind without any fear of going wrong. So many hours here, so many in the car, so many for you (he almost said). But no. Finally he was quite delicate in his manners. He would never have been able to say good-bye on his own. And anyway, we were bang in the middle, deep in high water, and no one would have dreamt of stopping to swim right now: not with the flat and the camp flowers and the prison windows.

For two days I tried to get rid of the musty smell in the rooms. He neither approved nor disapproved. We made love. Badly: it happens. The first time it never works, wherever you are. Nor when you change places. We made love in hotel rooms, in his car, in his office, once almost on a plane. This time it was terrible, and I blamed it on the light, a fastidious pink light that made my skin even paler than it really is and distracted me. He made love to me in silence, with his eyes closed. I began to imagine that he was dreaming other fantasies, and that made me feel even worse. We barely reached our climax. But there's something historical about inaugurating a house, however much rented it may be. I think we were happy when daylight turned from pink to blue to faded and then disappeared. He rose and dragged his thin, tender body through the room to the bathroom. I heard him whistle between his teeth and I almost got up. Almost immediately his hand landed on a thigh and then down, and forwards, until I gave in. I don't know how the devil he manages to caress a woman while keeping a poker-face. It's the sure-fire technique of the true professional; I mean: we were in love, past first base as it were. At first he seemed moved to the point of tears, and you would think he was suffering, but no. It's just that he takes these things very seriously, and stares into his woman's eyes with overpowering intensity.

To love and read and walk hand-in-hand through the pre-established points in the city. . . . Often he told me of his love. And I swear to God it could all be very pleasant. It had never really stopped being pleasant; I would have even made love once again, but it was getting late; I saw him dress and turn to the window that opened onto the back street. His house is on that street. I mean his real house. No nylon and no funny toilets that serve as ashtrays, I suppose. His real house; so when we first discussed the flat I argued that the location was absurd, so near, almost around the corner. I thought he'd draw back, but no.

"It's not a question of how far, my love," he explained.

I tried to show him that even if you were as cold-blooded as he was, this was not an *ordinary* situation. He answered with logic: love is never an ordinary situation.

"Two blocks away from your house," I insisted.

It really wasn't a question of distances. Did I think it became less important the further away it was? Well, in that case we'd end up making love in his living-room, or in the gallery next to the pool (I know the layout of his house, the place of his furniture, the order of his books, the room he sleeps in; I imagine it all). So while we made love, his wife would be making pottery. Or some other handicraft: they say it calms the nerves. I said *no* once more, but faintly, because with him I've always felt the fear of losing all (that "all" I haven't got; at least not *all*). With him I was always weak and full of anxiety.

"Fine, let's take the flat," I answered.

He gave me the keys, and then the flowers and the bit about love under the lights and a real home. I pointed to his real home trying to stir his conscience, but no. Moral anesthesia: that's clearly an aspect of his personality; also schizophrenia. And I was catching it too, naked thighs under his touch, watching the green facade of doubtful style. I could see the garage door, a bit of the first floor window, the stone border. I would see him come in and go out as if he had been placed in a rifle range. Bzzz, zap, bang, he would disappear, in the right-hand corner, there, got him in the middle, in the head with its youthful Roman air, the curly hair, the somewhat protruding bone beneath the eyebrows, bzzz zap, from the window of flat 604, sixth floor, like Kennedy, but with no crowds or CIA agents, nor policemen pushing Jackie, Jackie, poor thing, crawling away not to be hit, but here no Jackie nor CIA nor crowd not even a single miserable policeman: just the two of us, as always, in this madman's chatter that was love, of course it was, and then a woman aiming at a man with a gun. I could have, from the window—but no. I was staring at him again, now listless and peaceful, his lovely sex lying still after the cold water; staring at him—and then I saw once again the formidable look in his eyes, no love or hate, just sadness. I tried to find out if the greenish house outside my window depressed him or not. He put on the tie, the beige shirt. He sat on the stool, carefully brushing his thinning black hair. I remember I perched on the edge of the bed, naked, unhappy, not knowing what to do. He started to caress me again, and it all was as he had planned: very natural and painful. The daily sin—if it was a sin—was the same in sight of his house or on the Andes; a sin thirteen thousand kilometres away (for instance) is still a sin. But no.

The next few times were better and I grew accustomed to my life. I had breakfast in an elegant bar that would soon be broke because I was their only customer. I was respectfully called Madam; I would sip my coffee. I would wait for him at lunchtime after work; he would make short phone calls and when he heard my voice he'd let out a happy chuckle. Some time ago the chuckle meant hope, but no: now my situation was established, with the flat two blocks away from his house. (With the bedroom, the bathroom, the kitchen, with all these things that tied me to the wheel more effectively than any memory.) You are here, it all cried out. Even he said it one day: "You're here, established." He took it then for granted, my being there, and soon the janitor began to greet me affectionately, and I discovered an older woman, less shirty than the others at the back end of my floor, all kept there for identical reasons.

I tried to make the place look decent, and curiously, without giving up the unavoidable eyesores, it began to get better as the days went by. I almost stopped seeing the *camp* details. I managed to rip the nylon covers off the sofa on which we made exasperated love. I moved around two chairs, displaced a decorative soup tureen.

Every day I bought flowers from a fawning Indian woman, and I tried to accustom him to the same daily roses. I don't know whether he noticed them, but the roses lived out their circular lives with patient persistence: they grew large, they faded and died. Suddenly, in bed, he said: "I see your roses."

Through the window I learned to watch his comings and

goings. The car at the entrance: perhaps he's there. The car invisible: he's away. When he was with me he'd leave it at the end of the avenue that diagonally crosses his street. The car was a problem, he once admitted. But no. I never met anyone on my way out, no one ever saw us together. Every weekend was the same exaggerated torture. He'd disappear on Friday afternoon (because in this city people resurrect on Friday with a sort of perverse and contagious gregariousness) and I would find myself filling the two days ahead as actively as I could—those two days and a half of exile that at first drove me crazy. I sought out people, I made friends, I cooked meals and established relationships with other solitary souls like myself. From time to time a couple of lovers—still happy—visited me in the flat. Maybe they felt comforted in the house of a single woman, witnessing the opposite of happiness rather than peace. I actively filled my Friday nights, my long Saturdays, my warm faded Sundays. I smoked and drank like a Cossack. On Sunday mornings, seeing the state of my eyes and the swelling of the eyelids, I would drag myself back into bed wishing for death. But then I'd hear someone sing, and the furious barking of a dog, a dove, the cries from the street, the honking of horns. That is how I found out that Saturday morning is his day for family errands, and he lends himself to his duties with the gestures of a well-disposed schoolboy, anxious to please his teachers. In his blue T-shirt I would see him run down the steps of his house, walk to the car with rhythmical strides, with that drunkard's gait that is his own peculiar way of walking. I tried to make him look towards my window, but no. Come on, I would say, trying my hand at telepathy, parapsychology, whatever: look this way, think of me watching you, discover me here. He never did. One day his children appeared. An eight-year-old kid, his same head, his same nose. To tell the truth, of course no one can make out an eight-year-old's nose a block away. But I *swear* it was his hair, his nose. Of the four children who appeared and disappeared from time to time, the one with his nose was the one who made me sick.

I've already said somehere that one can give up a man, but almost never what could have been one's child. I felt sick when I went back for my whisky, but bucked up and arranged my four-thousandth invitation for that weekend: lunch at Status, movies at Pacifico, tea at La Sueca and dinner at Mariana's—who had also been his mistress. I would say to myself: a step away lies the same dejection, the same hysteria. But then Mariana never lived in a camp flat, never had him at the end of her gun: that was my privilege, and I was determined to defend it with enthusiasm. Mariana was only a warning and I went back to my post at the window feeling the urge to see him. Was I lucky, or not? I had discovered the fact that Saturday is a more "open" day than Sunday, and that Sunday can be borne with more comfort; after all, one is about to reach the time of Monday morning's phone call, and the *voice* on the phone.

We thought there'd be a break, but no. It was always wonderful to open the door, hesitate, find the thin body, those eyes I loved so much, the stubborn curls in his hair, and a smileless kiss, during and after the other, beautiful kisses. I vouch for that: his kisses were beautiful. Long kisses that arrived running from Friday night, before the forty-eight hours of wasteland. I haven't forgotten those kisses. Or we'd go out for a walk, barely down to the sea, there where the beach was dry and full of pebbles. Or to Barranca Gardens, where we'd visit the naked woman washing her hands in a fountain. You might think we lived like prisoners, but no. You acquire certain habits, discreet conventions through which the life-that-could-have-been can be peeked at. Like the way he flicks through books, caressing them; his loathing of German theorists; his lack of interest in any literature; and the jacket hung almost by chance on the back of a chair. I thought they were delightful habits.

The cheapest hairdresser in the area was Ruth and she would curl my hair in the camp style of the flat. He rarely noticed it but was fascinated by the moment of waiting, there, under the awning of camp curls in our shared surroundings. Soon I realized that I enjoyed living like this more than any other way I had lived before, and worse: that I would never outgrow it. You'd think he'd come to his senses, but no. He came and went harmoniously, correctly and cleanly: so many hours at work, so many hours at home, so many hours at the flat. He didn't stay long with me, some three hours, more or less. We'd fall asleep together; then I learnt that the best relationships take place in sleep. The bed acquired our smell. One exiled Saturday, however, it began raining early. I watched him come in and go out, put his children in the station wagon, and open the door for his wife. From a distance you discover things: for instance, that the boredom was true, as well as the sense of duty. I mean true, but not absolutely necessary. I also discovered that I was alive thanks to this man, and that the thanks would carry on for as long as he lived. But then there were times when he would not be with me; then the death in the heart would start once again, and the inability to live, and the obstacles, and so on until exhaustion.

He helped his wife to her seat, then settled his children. I must have looked away for a while; when I looked again the car had come back and I could no longer see the wife, only the children, the boy with the nose, and a thin girl with his same desolate expression. I saw him climb in, shopping bags on his shoulder, go back to the house, pile up three boxes, fetch more bags. With fascination, I saw him as he sees an insect under a generous glass which, rather than distorting it, makes it clearer, more precise, a color snapshot. My heart broke like a string that Saturday, as I remember it today, another Saturday, invited out, without him. I'll say that what bothered me most was the boy with the curious nose, that diabolical and innocent bit of himself. That child, for instance, would see him die.

The problem was that on Monday, when he came back, I enjoyed the kisses just as much as before. You might think something changed after my broken heart or the scene under the magnifying glass, but no. You might also think that he would realize his mistake. But no. After that otherwise happy Monday, I looked forward with anxiety to the end of the week, and I didn't even stare out of the window. I imagined him filling up the car and my heart broke again. Better this way, my love, I said grabbing the suitcase. Maybe I should have thought otherwise, but no. I leaned out and saw him edging the car down the driveway, I saw the thin body I enjoyed so much. Then I took with me two or three things, I put the monstrous objects back in their place, locked up the flat, and never saw that dearly loved man again.

Translated by Alberto Manguel

The Imitation
of the Rose

CLARICE LISPECTOR

Born in the Ukraine in 1922, Clarice Lispector arrived in Recife, Pernambuco, at the age of two months. She began writing short stories and plays while in her teens, before graduating from the National Law School in 1944. Like Dinah Silveira de Queiroz, another major Brazilian writer, she lived abroad with her husband, who was in the diplomatic service. In her work, Clarice Lispector recognizes the influence of the French existentialists. Her characters contemplate with despair their "freedom," their need to make a choice, and Clarice Lispector tells of their plight with a sharp almost ironical eye. Of all the Brazilian women writers, Clarice Lispector has perhaps been the most fortunate in finding her way into the English language. Several of her books are available in English, and a few of her stories have been admirably translated by the poet Elizabeth Bishop.

BEFORE ARMANDO CAME home from work the house would have to be tidied and Laura herself ready in her brown dress so that she could attend her husband while he dressed, and then they would leave at their leisure, arm in arm as in former times. How long was it since they had last done that?

But now that she was "well" again, they would take the bus, she looking like a wife, watching out of the bus window, her arm in his; and later they would dine with Carlota and João, sitting back intimately in their chairs. How long was it since she had seen Armando sit back with intimacy and talk with another man? A man at peace was one who, oblivious of his wife's presence, could talk with another man about the latest news in the headlines. Meanwhile, she would talk to Carlota about women's things, submissive to the authoritarian and practical goodness of Carlota, receiving once more her friend's attention and vague disdain, her natural abruptness, instead of that perplexed affection full of curiosity—watching Armando, finally oblivious of his own wife. And she herself, finally returning to play an insignificant role with gratitude. Like a cat which, having spent the night out of doors, as if nothing had happened, had unexpectedly found a saucer of milk waiting. People fortunately helped to make her feel that she was "well" again. Without watching her, they actively helped her to forget, they themselves feigning forgetfulness as if they had read the same directions on the same medicine bottle. Or, perhaps, they had really forgotten. How long was it since she last saw Armando sit back with abandon, oblivious of her presence? And she herself?

Interrupting her efforts to tidy up the dressing table, Laura gazed at herself in the mirror. And she herself? How long had it been? Her face had a domestic charm, her hair pinned behind her large pale ears. Her brown eyes and brown hair, her soft dark skin, all lent to that face, no longer so very young, the unassuming expression of a woman. Perhaps someone might have noticed in that ever so tiny hint of surprise in the depths of her eyes, perhaps someone might have seen in that ever so tiny hint of sorrow for the children she had never had?

With her punctilious liking for organization—that same inclination which had made her as a schoolgirl copy out her class notes in perfect writing without ever understanding them—to tidy up the house before the maid had her afternoon off so that, once Maria went out, she would have nothing more to do except (1) calmly get dressed; (2) wait for Armando once she was ready; (3) what was the third thing? Ah yes. That was exactly what she would do. She would wear her brown dress with the cream lace collar. Having already had her bath. . . . Even during her time at the Sacred Heart Convent she had always been tidy and clean, with an obsession for personal hygiene and a certain horror of disorder. A fact which never caused Carlota, who was already a little odd even as a school girl, to admire her. The reactions of the two women had always been different. Carlota, ambitious and laughing heartily; Laura, a little slow, and virtually always taking care to be slow. Carlota, seeing danger in nothing; and Laura, ever cautious. When they had given her *The Imitation of Christ* to read, with the zeal of a donkey she had gone through the book without understanding it, but may God forgive her, she had felt that anyone who imitated Christ would be lost—lost in the light, but dangerously lost. Christ was the worst temptation. And Carlota, who had not even attempted to read it, had lied to the Sister, saying that she had finished it.

It was decided. She would wear her brown dress with the cream collar made of real lace.

But when she saw the time, she remembered with alarm—causing her to raise her hand to her breast—that she had forgotten to drink her glass of milk.

She made straight for the kitchen and, as if she had guiltily betrayed Armando and their devoted friends through her neglect, standing by the refrigerator she took the first sips with anxious pauses, concentrating upon each one with something like faith, as if she were compensating everyone and showing her repentance.

When the doctor had said, "Take milk between your meals, and avoid an empty stomach because that causes anxiety," then, even without the threat of anxiety, she took her milk with no further discussion, sip by sip, day by day—she never failed, obeying blindly with a touch of zeal, so that she might not perceive in herself the slightest disbelief. The embarrassing thing was that the doctor appeared to contradict himself, for while giving precise instruction which she followed with the zeal of a convert, he had also said, "Relax! Take things easy; don't force yourself to succeed—completely forget what has happened and everything will return to normal." And he had given her a pat on the back that had pleased her and made her blush with pleasure.

But in her humble opinion, the one command seemed to cancel out the other, as if they were asking her to eat flour and whistle at the same time. In order to fuse both commands into one, she had invented a solution: that glass of milk which had finished up by gaining a secret power, which almost embodied with every sip the taste of a word and renewed that firm pat on the back, that glass of milk she carried into the sitting room where she sat "with great naturalness," feigning a lack of interest, "not forcing herself"—and thereby cleverly complying with the second order. It doesn't matter if I get fat, she thought, beauty has never been the most important thing.

She sat down on the couch as if she were a guest in her own home, which, so recently regained, tidy and impersonal, recalled the peace of a stranger's house. A feeling that gave her great satisfaction: the opposite of Carlota who had made her home something similar to herself, Laura experienced such pleasure in making something impersonal of her home. In a certain way it was perfect, because it was impersonal.

Oh, how good it was to be back, to be truly back, she smiled with satisfaction. Holding the almost empty glass, she closed her eyes with a pleasurable weariness. She had ironed Armando's shirts, she had prepared methodical lists for the following day, she had calculated in detail what she had spent at the market that morning; she had not paused, in fact, for a single minute. Oh, how good it was to be tired again!

If some perfect creature were to descend from the planet Mars and discover that people on the Earth were tired and growing old, he would feel pity and dismay. Without ever understanding what was good about being people, about feeling tired and failing daily. . . . Only the initiated would understand this nuance of depravity and refinement of life.

And she had returned at last from the perfection of the planet Mars. She, who had never had any ambitions except to be a wife to some man, gratefully returned to find her share of what is daily fallible. With her eyes closed she sighed her thanks. How long was it since she had felt tired? But now every day she'd felt almost exhausted. She had ironed, for example, Armando's shirts; she had always enjoyed ironing and, modesty aside, she pressed clothes to perfection. And afterward she felt exhausted as a sort of compensation. No longer to feel that alert lack of fatigue. No longer to feel that point—empty, aroused, and hideously exhilarating within oneself. No longer to feel that terrible independence. No longer that monstrous and simple facility of not sleeping—neither by day nor by night—which in her discretion had suddenly made her superhuman by comparison with her tired and perplexed husband. Armando, with that offensive breath which he developed when he was silently preoccupied, stir-

ring in her a poignant compassion, yes, even within her alert
perfection, her feeling and love . . . she, superhuman and
tranquil in her bright isolation, and he—when he had come
to visit her timidly bringing apples and grapes that the nurse,
with a shrug of her shoulders, used to eat—he visiting her
ceremoniously like a lover with heavy breath and fixed smile,
forcing himself in his heroism to try to understand . . . he
who had received her from a father and a clergyman, and
who did not know what to do with this girl from Tijuca, who
unexpectedly, like a tranquil boat spreading its sails over the
water, had become superhuman.

But now it was over. All over. Oh, it had been a mere
weakness: temperament was the worst temptation. But later
she had recovered so completely that she had even started
once more to exercise care not to plague others with her
former obsession for detail. She could well remember her
companions at the convent saying to her, "That's the thou-
sandth time you've counted that!" She remembered them
with an uneasy smile.

She had recovered completely and now she was tired every
day, every day her face sagged as the afternoon wore on, and
the night then assumed its old finality and became more than
just a perfect starry night. Everything completed itself harmoniously. And, as for the whole world, each day fatigued
her; as for the whole world, human and perishable. No longer
that thing which one day had clearly spread like a cancer . . .
her soul.

She opened her eyes heavy with sleep, feeling the consoling
solidity of the glass in her hand, but closed them again with a
comfortable smile of fatigue, bathing herself like a *nouveau
riche* in all his wealth, in this familiar and slightly nauseating
water. Yes, slightly nauseating; what did it matter? For if she,
too, was a little nauseating, she was fully aware of it. But her
husband didn't think so and then what did it matter, for hap-

pily she did not live in surroundings which demanded that she should be more clever and interesting; she was even free of school which so embarrassingly had demanded that she should be alert. What did it matter? In exhaustion—she had ironed Armando's shirts without mentioning that she had been to the market in the morning and had spent some time there with that delight she took in making things yield—in exhaustion she found a refuge, that discreet and obscure place from where, with so much constraint toward herself and others, she had once departed. But as she was saying, fortunately she had returned.

And if she searched with greater faith and love she would find within her exhaustion that even better place, which would be sleep. She sighed with pleasure, for one moment of mischievous malice tempted to go against that warm breath she exhaled, already inducing sleep . . . for one moment tempted to doze off. "Just for a moment, only one tiny moment!" she pleaded with herself, pleased at being so tired, she pleaded persuasively, as one pleads with a man, a facet of her behaviour that had always delighted Armando. But she did not really have time to sleep now, not even to take a nap, she thought smugly and with false modesty. She was such a busy person! She had always envied those who could say "I couldn't find the time," and now once more she was such a busy person.

They were going to dinner at Carlota's house, and everything had to be organized and ready, it was her first dinner out since her return and she did not wish to arrive late, she had to be ready. "Well, I've already said this a thousand times," she thought with embarrassment. It would be sufficient to say it only once. "I did not wish to arrive late." For this was a sufficient reason: if she had never been able to bear without enormous vexation giving trouble to anyone, now more than ever, she should not. No, no, there was not the slightest doubt: she had no time to sleep. What she must do, stirring herself with familiarity in that intimate wealth of routine—and it hurt her that Carlota should despise her liking for routine—what she must do was (1) wait until the maid was ready; (2) give her the money so that she could bring the meat in the morning, topside of beef, how could she explain that the difficulty of finding good meat was, for her, really an interesting topic of conversation, but if Carlota were to find out, she would despise her; (3) to begin washing and dressing herself carefully, surrendering without reservations to the pleasure of making the most of the time at her disposal. Her brown dress matched her eyes, and her collar in cream lace gave her an almost childlike appearance, like some child from the past. And, back in the nocturnal peace of Tijuca, no longer that dazzling light of ebullient nurses, their hair carefully set, going out to enjoy themselves after having tossed her like a helpless chicken into the void of insulin—back to the nocturnal peace of Tijuca, restored to her real life.

She would go out arm in arm with Armando, walking slowly to the bus stop with those low thick hips which her girdle parceled into one, transforming her into a striking woman. But when she awkwardly explained to Armando that this resulted from ovarian insufficiency, Armando, who liked his wife's hips, would saucily retort, "What good would it do me to be married to a ballerina?" That was how he responded. No one would have suspected it, but at times Armando could be extremely devious. From time to time they repeated the same phrases. She explained that it was on account of ovarian insufficiency. Then he would retort, "What good would it do me to be married to a ballerina?" At times he was shameless and no one would have suspected it.

Carlota would have been horrified if she were to know that they, too, had an intimate life and shared things she could not discuss, but nevertheless she regretted not being able to discuss them. Carlota certainly thought that she was merely neat and ordinary and a little boring; but if she were obliged to take care in order not to annoy the others with details, with Armando she let herself go at times and became boring. Not that this mattered because, although he pretended to listen, he did not absorb everything she told him. Nor did she take offense, because she understood perfectly well that her conversation rather bored other people, but it was nice to be able to tell him that she had been able to find good meat, even if Armando shook his head and did not listen. She and the maid talked a good deal, in fact more so she than the maid, and she was careful not to bother the maid, who at times could not suppress her impatience and became somewhat rude— the fault was really hers because she did not always command respect.

But, as she was saying . . . her arm in his, she short and he tall and thin, though he was healthy, thank God, and she was chestnut-haired. Chestnut-haired as she obscurely felt a wife ought to be. To have black or blonde hair was an exaggeration, which, in her desire to make the right choice, she had never wanted. Then, as for green eyes, it seemed to her that if she had green eyes it would be as if she had not told her husband everything. Not that Carlota had given any cause for scandal, although Laura, were she given the opportunity, would hotly defend her, but the opportunity had never arisen. She, Laura, was obliged reluctantly to agree that her friend had a strange and amusing way of treating her husband, not because "they treated each other as equals," since this was now common enough, but you know what I mean. . . . And Carlota was even a little different, even she had remarked on this once to Armando, and Armando had agreed without attaching much importance to the fact. But, as she was saying, in brown with the lace collar . . . her reverie filled her with the same pleasure she experienced when tidying up drawers, and she even found herself disarranging them in order to tidy them up again.

She opened her eyes and, as if it were the room that had taken a nap and not she, the room seemed refurbished and refreshed with its chairs brushed and its curtains, which had shrunk in the last washing, looking like trousers that are too short and the wearer looking comically at his own legs. Oh! how good it was to see everything tidy again and free of dust, everything cleaned by her own capable hands, and so silent and with a vase of flowers as in a waiting room. She had always found waiting rooms pleasing, so respectful and impersonal. How satisfying life together was, for her who had at last returned from extravagance. Even a vase of flowers. She looked at it.

"Ah! how lovely they are," her heart exclaimed suddenly, a bit childish. They were small wild roses which she had bought that morning at the market, partly because the man had insisted so much, partly out of daring. She had arranged them in a vase that very morning, while drinking her sacred glass of milk at ten o'clock.

But in the light of this room the roses stood in all their complete and tranquil beauty. "Have I ever seen such lovely roses?" she thought enquiringly. And, as if she had not just been thinking precisely this, vaguely aware that she had been thinking precisely this, and quickly dismissing her embarrassment upon recognizing herself as being a little tedious, she thought in a newer phase of surprise, "Really, I have never seen such pretty roses." She looked at them attentively. But her attention could not be sustained for very long as simple attention, and soon transformed itself into soothing pleasure, and she was no longer able to analyze the roses and felt obliged to interrupt herself with the same exclamation of submissive enquiry: "How lovely they are!"

They were a bouquet of perfect roses, several on the same

stem. Once they had climbed with quick eagerness over each other but then, their game over, they had become calmly immobilized. They were quite perfect roses in their minuteness, not quite open, and their pink hue was almost white. "They seem almost artificial," she uttered in surprise. They might give the impression of being white if they were completely open, but with the centre petals curled in a bud, their colour was concentrated and, as in the lobe of an ear, one could sense the redness circulate inside them. "How lovely they are," thought Laura, surprised. But without knowing why, she felt somewhat restrained and a little perplexed. Oh, nothing serious, it was only that such extreme beauty disturbed her.

She heard the maid's footsteps on the brick floor of the kitchen, and from the hollow sound she realized that she was wearing high heels and that she must be ready to leave. Then Laura had an idea which was in some way highly original: why not ask Maria to call at Carlota's house and leave the roses as a present?

And also because that extreme beauty disturbed her. Disturbed her? It was a risk. Oh! no, why a risk? It merely disturbed her; they were a warning. Oh! no, why a warning? Maria would deliver the roses to Carlota.

"Dona Laura sent them," Maria would say. She smiled thoughtfully: Carlota would be puzzled that Laura, being able to bring the roses personally, since she wanted to present them to her, should send them before dinner with the maid. Not to mention that she would find it amusing to receive the roses . . . and would think it "refined."

"These things aren't necessary between us, Laura!" the other would say with that frankness of hers which was somewhat tactless, and Laura would exclaim in a subdued cry of rapture, "Oh, no! no! It is not because of the invitation to dinner! It is because the roses are so lovely that I felt the impulse to give them to you!"

Yes, if at the time the opportunity arose and she had the courage, that was exactly what she would say. What exactly would she say? It was important not to forget. She would say, "Oh, no! no! It is not because of the invitation to dinner! It is because the roses are so lovely that I felt the impulse to give them to you!"

And Carlota would be surprised at the delicacy of Laura's sentiments—no one would imagine that Laura, too, had her ideas. In this imaginary and pleasurable scene which made her smile devoutly, she addressed herself as "Laura," as if speaking to a third person. A third person full of that gentle, rustling, pleasant, and tranquil faith, Laura, the one with the real lace collar, dressed discreetly, the wife of Armando, an Armando, after all, who no longer needed to force himself to pay attention to all of her conversation about the maid and the meat . . . who no longer needed to think about his wife, like a man who is happy, like a man who is not married to a ballerina.

"I couldn't help sending you the roses," Laura would say, this third person so, but so. . . . And to give the roses was almost as nice as the roses themselves.

And she would even be rid of them.

And what exactly would happen next? Ah yes: as she was saying, Carlota, surprised at Laura who was neither intelligent nor good but who had her secret feelings. And Armando? Armando would look at her with a look of real surprise—for it was essential to remember that he must not know the maid had taken the roses in the afternoon! Armando would look with kindness upon the impulses of his little wife and that night they would sleep together.

And she would have forgotten the roses and their beauty. No, she suddenly thought, vaguely warned. It was necessary to take care with that alarmed look in others. It was necessary never to cause them alarm, especially with everything being so fresh in their minds. And, above all, to spare everyone the least anxiety or doubt. And that the attention of others should no longer be necessary—no longer this horrible feeling of their watching her in silence, and her in their presence. No more impulses.

But at the same time she saw the empty glass in her hand and she also thought, " 'He' said that I should not force myself to succeed, that I should not think of adopting attitudes merely to show that I am."

"Maria," she called, upon hearing her maid's footsteps once more. And when Maria appeared she asked with a note of rashness and defiance, "Would you call at Dona Carlota's house and leave these roses for her? Just say that Dona Laura sent them. Just say it like that. Dona Laura. . . ."

"Yes, I know," the maid interrupted her impatiently.

Laura went in search of an old sheet of tissue paper. Then she carefully lifted the roses from the vase, so lovely and tranquil, with their delicate and mortal thorns. She wanted to make a really artistic bouquet: and at the same time she would be rid of them. And she would be able to dress and resume her day. When she had arranged the moist blooms in a bouquet, she held the flowers away from her and examined them at a distance, slanting her head and half-closing her eyes for an impartial and severe judgement.

And when she looked at them, she saw the roses. And then, irresistibly gentle, she insinuated to herself, "Don't give the roses away, they are so lovely."

A second later, still very gently, her thought suddenly became slightly more intense, almost tempting, "Don't give them away, they are yours." Laura became a little frightened: because things were never hers.

But these roses were. Tinged with red, small, and perfect: they were hers. She looked at them, incredulous: they were beautiful and they were hers. If she could think further ahead, she would think: hers as nothing before now had ever been.

And she could even keep them because that initial uneasiness had passed which had caused her vaguely to avoid looking at the roses too much.

"Why give them away then? They are so lovely and you are giving them away? So when you find something nice, you just go and give it away? Well, if they were hers," she insinuated persuasively to herself, without finding any other argument beyond the previous one which, when repeated, seemed to her to be ever more convincing and straightforward.

"They would not last long—why give them away then, so long as they are alive?" The pleasure of possessing them did not represent any great risk, she pretended to herself, because, whether she liked it or not, shortly she would be forced to deprive herself of them and then she would no longer think about them, because by then they would have withered.

"They would not last long; why give them away then?" The fact that they would not last long seemed to free her from the guilt of keeping them, in the obscure logic of the woman who sins. Well, one could see that they would not last long (it would be sudden, without danger). And it was not even, she argued in a final and victorious rejection of guilt, she herself who had wanted to buy them; the florist had insisted so much and she always became so intimidated when they argued with her. . . . It was not she who had wanted to buy them . . . she was not to blame in the slightest. She looked at them in rapture, thoughtful and profound.

"And, honestly, I never saw such perfection in all my life."

All right, but she had already spoken to Maria and there would be no way of turning back. Was it too late then? She became frightened upon seeing the tiny roses that waited impassively in her own hand. If she wanted, it would not be too late. . . . She could say to Maria, "Oh, Maria, I have decided to take the roses myself when I go to dinner this evening!" And of course she would not take them. . . . And Maria need never know. And, before changing, she would sit on her couch for a moment, just for a moment, to contemplate them. To contemplate that tranquil impassivity of the roses. Yes, because having already done the deed, it would be better to profit from it . . . she would not be foolish enough to take the blame without the profit. That was exactly what she would do.

But with the roses unwrapped in her hand she waited. She did not arrange them in the vase, nor did she call Maria. She knew why. Because she must give them away. Oh, she knew why.

And also because something nice was either for giving or receiving, not only for possessing. And above all, never for one *to be*. Above all one should never *be* a lovely thing. A lovely thing lacked the gesture of giving. One should never keep a lovely thing, as if it were guarded within the perfect silence of one's heart. (Although, if she were not to give the roses, would anyone ever find out? It was horribly easy and within one's reach to keep them, for who would find out? And they would be hers, and things would stay as they were and the matter would be forgotten. . . .)

"Well then? Well then?" she mused, vaguely disturbed.

Well, no. What she must do was to wrap them up and send them, without any pleasure now; to parcel them up and, disappointed, send them; and, terrified, be rid of them. Also, because a person had to be coherent, one's thoughts had to be consistent; if, spontaneously, she had decided to relinquish them to Carlota, she would stand by the decision and give them away. For people didn't change their minds from one minute to another.

But anyone can repent, she suddenly rebelled. For if it was only the minute I took hold of the roses that I noticed how lovely they were, for the first time, actually, as I held them, I noticed how lovely they were. Or a little before that? (And they were really hers.) And even the doctor himself had patted her on the back and said, "Don't force yourself into pre-

tending that you are well, because you *are* well!" And then
that hearty pat on the back. So she was not obliged, therefore, to be consistent, she didn't have to prove anything to
anyone, and she would keep the roses. (And in all sincerity—
in all sincerity they were hers.)

"Are they ready?" Maria asked.

"Yes," said Laura, surprised.

She looked at them so mute in her hand. Impersonal in
their extreme beauty. In their extreme and perfect tranquility
as roses. That final instance: the flower. That final perfection;
its luminous tranquility.

Like someone depraved, she watched with vague longing
the tempting perfection of the roses . . . with her mouth a
little dry, she watched them.

Until, slowly, austerely, she wrapped the stems and thorns
in the tissue paper. She was so absorbed that only upon holding out the bouquet she had prepared did she notice that
Maria was no longer in the room—and she remained alone
with her heroic sacrifice.

Vacantly, sorrowfully, she watched them, distant as they
were at the end of her outstretched arm—and her mouth
became even dryer, parched by that envy and desire.

"But they are mine," she said with enormous timidity.

When Maria turned and took hold of the bouquet, for one
tiny moment of greed Laura drew back her hand, keeping the
roses to herself for one more second—they are so lovely and
they are mine—the first lovely thing and mine! And it was the
florist who had insisted . . . I did not go looking for them! It
was destiny that had decreed! Oh, only this once! Only this
once and I swear never more! (She could at least take one
rose for herself, no more than this. One rose for herself. And
only she would know and then never more; oh, she promised
herself that never more would she allow herself to be tempted
by perfection, never more.)

And the next moment, without any transition, without any

obstacle, the roses were in the maid's hand, they were no longer hers, like a letter already in the post! One can no longer recover or obliterate statements! There is no point in shouting, "That was not what I wanted to say!" Her hands were now empty but her heart, obstinate and resentful, was still saying, "You can catch Maria on the stairs, you know perfectly well that you can, and take the roses from her hand and steal them—because to take them now would be to steal them." To steal what was hers? For this was what a person without any feeling for others would do: he would steal what was his by right! Have pity, dear God. You can get them back, she insisted, enraged. And then the front door slammed.

Slowly, she sat down calmly on the couch. Without leaning back. Only to rest. No, she was no longer angry, not even a little. But that tiny wounded spot in the depths of her eyes was larger and thoughtful. She looked at the vase.

"Where are my roses?" she said then very quietly.

And she missed the roses. They had left an empty space inside her. Remove an object from a clean table and by the cleaner patch which remains one sees that there has been dust all around it. The roses had left a patch without dust and without sleep inside her. In her heart, that one rose, which at least she could have taken for herself without prejudicing anyone in the world, was gone. Like something missing. Indeed, like some great loss. An absence that flooded into her like a light. And also around the mark left by the roses the dust was disappearing. The centre of fatigue opened itself into a circle that grew larger. As if she had not ironed a single shirt for Armando. And in the clearing they had left, one missed those roses.

"Where are my roses?" she moaned without pain, smoothing the pleats of her skirt.

Like lemon juice dripping into dark tea and the dark tea becoming completely clear, her exhaustion gradually became clearer. Without, however, any tiredness. Just as the firefly alights. Since she was no longer tired, she was on the point of getting up to dress. It was time to start getting ready.

With parched lips, she tried for an instant to imitate the roses deep down inside herself. It was not even difficult.

It was just as well that she did not feel tired. In this way she would go out to dinner feeling more refreshed. Why not wear her cameo brooch on her cream-coloured collar? The one the Major had brought back from the war in Italy. It would add a final touch to her neckline. When she was ready she would hear the noise of Armando's key in the door. She must get dressed. But it was still early. With the rush-hour traffic, he would be late in arriving. It was still afternoon. An extremely beautiful afternoon. But, in fact, it was no longer afternoon. It was evening. From the street there arose the first sounds of darkness and the first lights.

Moreover, the key penetrated with familiarity the keyhole.

Armando would open the door. He would press the light switch. And suddenly in the frame of the doorway that face would appear, betraying an expectancy he tried to conceal but could not restrain. Then his breathless suspense would finally transform itself into a smile of utter relief. That embarrassed smile of relief which he would never suspect her of noticing. That relief which, probably with a pat on the back, they had advised her poor husband to conceal. But which had been, for this woman whose heart was filled with guilt, her daily recompense for having restored to her husband the possibility of happiness and peace, sanctified at the hands of an austere priest who only permitted submissive happiness to humans and not the imitation of Christ.

The key turned in the lock, that dark, expectant face entered, and a powerful light flooded the room.

And in the doorway, Armando himself stopped short with that breathless expression as if he had run for miles in order to arrive in time. She was about to smile. So that she might dispel the anxious expectancy on his face, which always came mixed with the childish victory of having arrived in time to find his boring, good-hearted, and diligent wife. She was about to smile so that once more he might know that there would no longer be any danger in his arriving too late. She was about to smile in order to teach him gently to confide in her. It had been useless to advise them never to touch on the subject; they did not speak about it but they had created a language of facial expressions whereby fear and confidence were communicated, and question and answer were silently telegraphed. She was about to smile. She was taking her time, but meant to smile.

Calmly and sweetly she said, "It came back, Armando. It came back."

As if he would never understand, he averted his smiling, distrusting face. His main task for the moment was to try and control his breathless gasps after running up the stairs, now that, triumphantly, he had arrived in time, now that she was there to smile at him. As if he would never understand.

"What came back?" he finally asked her in an expressionless tone.

But while he was seeking never to understand, the man's face, ever more full of suspense, had already understood without a single feature having altered. His main task was to gain time and to concentrate upon controlling his breath. Which suddenly was no longer difficult. For unexpectedly he noticed to his horror that the room and the woman were calm and showing no signs of haste. Still more suspicious, like someone about to end up howling with laughter upon observing something absurd, he meantime insisted upon keeping his face averted, from where he spied at her cautiously, almost her enemy. And from where he already began to feel unable to restrain himself, from seeing her seated with her hands folded upon her lap, with the serenity of the firefly that is alight.

In her innocent, chestnut gaze, the embarrassed vanity of not having been able to resist.

"What came back?" he asked suddenly with severity.

"I couldn't help myself," she said and her final compassion for this man was in her voice, one last appeal for pardon which already came mingled with the arrogance of an almost perfect solitude.

"I couldn't prevent it," she repeated, surrendering to him with relief the compassion which she with some effort had been able to contain until he arrived.

"It was on account of the roses," she said modestly.

As if a photograph were about to capture that moment, he still maintained the same disinterested expression, as if the photographer had asked him only for his face and not his soul. He opened his mouth and involuntarily his face took on for an instant an expression of comic detachment which he had used to conceal his annoyance when he had asked his boss for an increase in salary. The next moment, he averted his eyes, mortified by his wife's shamelessness as she sat there unburdened and serene.

But suddenly the tension fell. His shoulders dropped, the features of his face relaxed and a great heaviness settled over him. Aged and strange, he watched her.

She was seated wearing her little housedress. He knew that she had done everything possible not to become luminous and remote. With fear and respect he watched her. Aged, tired, and strange. But he did not even have a word to offer. From the open door he saw his wife sitting upright on the couch, once more alert and tranquil as if on a train. A train that had already departed.

Translated by Giovanni Pontiero

Guidance

DINAH SILVEIRA DE QUEIROZ

*THE LANDSCAPE OF Brazil is less apparent in the stories of
Dinah Silveira de Queiroz than in those of many of her con-
temporaries. Her experience comes from abroad, from Europe
and the United States, where she lived with her husband in
the diplomatic service, and the eye she casts upon her characters reminds the reader of the early Chekhov. "I write," she
once said, "about people, men and women, who happen to
live in my country and who happen to speak my tongue. But
I have not necessarily known them: sometimes I've met their
cousins, aunts, brothers, sisters in Africa, in Paris, in New
York. I dislike local colour." Of her many novels, novellas,
two plays, and children's books, the best is perhaps her collection of short stories,* As Noites do Morro do Encanto *(Nights
on the Mountain of Wonders), published in 1957, from
which the following story is taken.*

WHEN PEOPLE TALK to me about virtue, about morality and immorality, about deportment, about anything, in short, that has to do with right and wrong, I see Mama in my mind's eye. Not exactly Mama. Just Mama's neck, her white, tremulous throat, as she was enjoying one of her giggles. They sounded like someone delicately sipping coffee from a saucer. She used to laugh this way chiefly at night when, with just the three of us in the house, she would come to the dinner table in one of her gay, loose, low-necked gowns as if she were going to a ball. She would be so perfumed that the objects around her developed a little atmosphere of their own and became lighter and more delicate. She never used rouge or lipstick, but she must have done something to her skin to get that smoothness of freshly washed china. On her, even perspiration was lovely, like moisture on clear glass. Before such beauty, my face was a miserable and busy topography, where I would explore furiously, and with physical enjoyment, little underground caves in the deep, dark pores, or tiny volcanoes which, to my pleasure, would burst between my nails. Mama's laugh was a "thank you so much" to my father, who used to flatter her as if his life depended on her good will. He tried, however, to conceal this adulation by joking and by treating her eternally as a child. A long time before, a woman spiritualist had said something that certainly must have provoked her very best and special giggle:

"Why don't you try to exert a moral influence on people? You don't realize it, but you have an extraordinary power over others. You should go in for counselling. People sense your authority as soon as they meet you. Give guidance. Your advice will never fail. It comes from your mediumistic power. . . ."

Mama repeated this four or five times among her lady friends and the idea caught on, in our town of Laterra.

If someone was contemplating a business transaction, you

can be sure he'd show up at our house to get advice. On these occasions Mama, who was blonde and petite, seemed to grow taller and very erect, with her little head high and her chubby fingers upraised. They used to consult Mama about politics and about marriages. Because everything she said was sensible and turned out to be correct, they began also to send wayward persons to her. Once a certain rich lady brought her son, an incorrigible drunkard. I remember Mama said the most beautiful things about the reality of the Devil and about having to side with either the Beast or the Angel. She explained the misery in which the young man was foundering and scolded him with tremendous words. Her fat little finger was poised threateningly and her whole body trembled in righteous anger, although her voice was not raised above its natural tone. The young man and the lady wept together.

Papa was enchanted with the prestige which, as her husband, he enjoyed.

Quarrels between employer and employee, between husband and wife, between parents and children, all found their way to our house.

Mama would hear both sides, would advise, would moralize. And Papa, in his little shop, felt the influx of confidence spreading to his dominion.

It was at this time that Laterra found itself without a priest, for the vicar had died and the bishop had not yet sent a replacement. The townspeople had to go to San Antonio to get married or to baptize their children. But, for their novenas and their beads, they relied on my mother. Suddenly everyone became more religious. She would go to evening prayer in a lace veil, so fragrant and smooth of skin, so pure of face, that everybody said she looked like, and indeed was, a real saint. Untrue: a saint would not have emitted those little giggles, a saint would not have had so much fun. Fun is a sort of insult to the unhappy, and that is why Mama laughed and enjoyed herself only when we were alone.

One day, at the market fair in Laterra, a yokel asked:

"They say you got a lady priest here. Where does she live?"

Mama was told about it. She did not laugh.

"I don't like that." And she added: "I never was a religious fanatic. I'm just a normal person who wants to help her neighbour. If they go on with that kind of talk, I'll never take out my beads again."

But that very night, I saw her throat tremble with delight:

"Now they're calling me a lady priest. . . . Imagine!"

She had found her vocation. And she continued to give advice, to say fine things, to console those who had lost their loved ones. Once, on the birthday of a man whose child she had godmothered, Mama said such beautiful words about old age, about the flight of time, about the good we should do before night falls, that the man asked:

"Why don't you give a talk like this every Sunday? We have no vicar and the young people need guidance. . . ."

Everyone thought it an excellent idea. A society was founded, the Laterra Parents' Circle, which had its meetings at the city hall. People came from far away to hear Mama speak. Everybody said that she did an enormous amount of good to people's souls, that the sweetness of her words comforted those who were suffering. A number of individuals were converted by her. I think my father believed in her more than anyone else did. But I couldn't think of my mother as a predestined being, come to the world just to do good. It seemed to me that she was playacting and I felt a little ashamed. But at the same time I asked myself:

"Why should you feel this way? Doesn't she reconcile couples who have separated, doesn't she console widows, doesn't she even correct the incorrigible?"

One day, at lunchtime, Mama said to my father:

"Today they brought me a difficult case. . . . A strange young man. You're going to give him work. Just for the love of God. He came asking for help . . . and I must not turn him away. The poor boy cried so, he implored me . . . telling about his terrible problem. He's wretched!"

A dream of glory enticed her:

"Do you know that the doctors in San Antonio could do nothing for him? I want you to help me. I think it's important for him to work . . . here. It will cost you nothing. He says he wants to work for us free because he knows that I don't accept payment for my work either and do everything just out of kindness."

The new employee looked like a pretty girl. He was rosy-cheeked, had dark eyes with long lashes, moved about without making the least noise. He knew some poetry by heart and sometimes recited it in a soft voice while cleaning the counter in the store. When people learned that he was employed by us, they advised my father:

"This isn't the kind of person to work in a respectable house!"

"She wanted it," replied my father. "She always knows what she's doing."

The new employee worked with a will, but he had crises of anxiety. Although it was agreed that he would dine with us, on certain nights he did not do so. And he would appear later with his eyes red.

Many times, Mama shut herself in the living room with him and her quiet voice scolded and wounded him. She would also correct him before my father and even before me, but smiling with kindness:

"Take your hand away from your waist. You look like a girl, and if you act this way, then . . ."

But she knew how to say things that he surely wanted to hear:

"There is no one better than you on this earth! Why are you afraid of other people? Come on, lift up your head!"

Stimulated by this, my father guaranteed:

"In my house no one will ever insult you. I'd just like to see someone try!"

No one ever did. Even the boys in the street, who used to point at him and talk loudly and laugh, became serious and fled as soon as my father appeared at the door.

And for a long time the young man was never absent from dinner. In his leisure hours he made pretty things for Mama. He painted a fan for her and made a jar in the form of a swan, out of old, wet paper, glue, and heaven knows what. He became my friend. He knew about clothes and styles as nobody else did. He would express opinions about my dresses. At the hour of prayer he, who had been so humiliated, whose look had been that of a beaten creature, now would come and take a place next to Mama, with a chaplet in his hand. If visitors called while he was with us, he did not scurry away as he had previously done. He remained in a corner, looking at everyone calmly and amicably. I watched his gradual metamorphosis. Less timid, he had become less effeminate. His movements were more confident, his physical attitudes less ridiculous.

Mama, who had carefully watched her conversation when he was present, now virtually forgot that he was not one of us. She would laugh freely, with her delightful, tremulous giggles. She seemed to have stopped teaching him how to behave, for it was no longer necessary. And he, when not at the counter, began to follow her about. He helped her in the house, he went shopping with her. Mama had reproved certain young women for their love intrigues; seeing her pass by they would say, hidden behind their windows:

"Don't you think maybe she's cured him . . . too much?"

Laterra took pride in Mama, the most important person in the community. It pained many persons to observe that almost comical affection. They would see her walk by quickly, erect, with firm step, and the young man behind, carrying her packages, or at her side, holding her parasol with a certain fervour as if it had been a pallium in a religious procession. An obvious restlessness pervaded the city. It reached such a point that one Sunday, when Mama was talking on conjugal happiness and the duties of marriage, some heads turned toward the young man, almost imperceptibly but enough for me to perceive their thought. And an absurd feeling of forboding oppressed my heart.

Mama was the last to become aware of the passion she had aroused.

"Look," she said, "I only tried to build up his morale. . . . His own mother gave him up as lost—she even wished him dead! And today he's a fine young man! I'm only saying what everybody knows."

Papa was becoming despondent. One day he got it off his chest:

"I think it's better if he leaves. Obviously, you've succeeded in what you were trying to do. You've made him decent and hard-working, like anybody else. Let's thank God and send him back home. You did a wonderful job!"

"But," said Mama in amazement, "don't you see that more time is needed . . . so they'll forget about him? To send this boy back now would be a sin! A sin that I don't want on my conscience."

There was one night when the young man told a story at dinner about a hillbilly. Mama laughed as she had never laughed before, throwing back her petite head, showing her most disturbing nudity—her neck—with that tremulous chirp of hers. I saw his face become red and his eyes shine at the sight of her white splendour. Papa did not laugh. I felt unhappy and frightened. Three days later the young man fell ill with a grippe. It was while Mama was visiting him in his room that he said something to her. I'll never know what it was. For the first time, we heard Mama raise her voice. It was loud, strident, furious. A week later he was well and resumed work. She said to my father:

"You're right. It's time for him to go back home."

At dinner hour Mama told the maidservant:

"We'll be the only ones tonight. Just set three places. . . ."

The next day, at the hour of prayer, the young man arrived in a state of fear, but he came along and took his usual place next to Mama.

"Go away!" she said in a low voice before beginning the prayer. He obeyed, not even pleading with his eyes.

Every head slowly followed him. I watched him, with his unobtrusive, school-girl walk, going out into the night.

In a few moments Mama's voice, slightly tremulous, was praying:

"Our Father who art in heaven, hallowed be Thy name. . . ."

The voices that accompanied hers were stronger than they had been in many days.

He did not return to his own town, where he had been the accepted object of ridicule. That very night a farmer, on leaving Laterra, saw a long shape swinging from a tree. He thought it might be an assailant, but he courageously approached the figure. He discovered the young man. We were called. I saw him. Mama didn't. By the light of the lantern he seemed more ridiculous than tragic . . . so frail, hanging there like a Judas with a face of purple cloth. An enormous crowd soon encircled the mango tree. I was convinced that all of Laterra was breathing easier. Now it had proof! Its lady had not transgressed, its moralist had not failed it.

For several months Mama, perfect and perfumed as always, uttered none of her giggles, although she continued, now without great conviction (I could tell), to give guidance. Even at dinner she wore dark dresses, closed at the neck.

Translated by William L. Grossman

The Bloody Countess

ALEJANDRA PIZARNIK

SURREALISM, WHICH SEEMS to have had an almost secret influence on Canadian or North American writers, was vigorously important in many Latin American countries, especially in Argentina, where the poet Aldo Pellegrini founded the surrealist magazine Qué in the late twenties, thereby providing new writers with a publication that gave coherence to the movement. One of the finest, most original of surrealist poets was Alejandra Pizarnik. A trip to Paris in the late fifties led her to discover the writings of André Pieyre de Mandiargues and Georges Bataille and to renew her friendship with Julio Cortázar. She returned to Buenos Aires to write tiny, closely cropped poems, which she would try out on a small blackboard, dusting out words until she was left with barely a line or two, the core of a vaster, inexistent work. For instance:

> And it is always the far bank of the river.
> If the soul asks, Is it far?, you shall answer:
> On the far bank of the river. Not this one, but the next.

Alejandra Pizarnik admired Borges's ability to combine essays and short stories in his ficciones (she could recite The Wall and the Books by heart), and her only prose piece, "The Bloody Countess," seemingly a book review or article, is in fact a tale in the tradition Borges had established. Alejandra Pizarnik committed suicide in 1972.

> The criminal does not make beauty;
> he himself is the authentic beauty.
> JEAN-PAUL SARTRE

THERE IS A BOOK by Valentine Penrose which documents the life of a real and unusual character: the Countess Bathory, murderer of more than six hundred young girls. The Countess Bathory's sexual perversion and her madness are so obvious that Valentine Penrose disregards them and concentrates instead on the convulsive beauty of the character.

It is not easy to show this sort of beauty. Valentine Penrose, however, succeeded because she played admirably with the aesthetic value of this lugubrious story. She inscribes the underground kingdom of Erzebet Bathory within the walls of her torture chamber, and the chamber within her medieval castle. Here the sinister beauty of nocturnal creatures is summed up in this silent lady of legendary paleness, mad eyes, and hair the sumptuous colour of ravens.

A well-known philosopher includes cries in the category of silence—cries, moans, curses, form "a silent substance." The substance of this underworld is evil. Sitting on her throne, the countess watches the tortures and listens to the cries. Her old and horrible maids are wordless figures that bring in fire, knives, needles, irons; they torture the girls, and later bury them. With their iron and knives, these two old women are themselves the instruments of a possession. This dark ceremony has a single silent spectator.

I. The Iron Maiden

> . . . among red laughter of glistening lips and
> monstrous gestures of mechanical women.
> RENÉ DAUMAL

THERE WAS ONCE in Nuremberg a famous automaton known as the Iron Maiden. The Countess Bathory bought a copy for her torture chamber in Csejthe Castle. This clockwork doll was of the size and colour of a human creature. Naked, painted, covered in jewels, with blond hair that reached down to the ground, it had a mechanical device that allowed it to curve its lips into a smile, and to move its eyes.

The Countess, sitting on her throne, watches.

For the Maiden to spring into action it is necessary to touch some of the precious stones in its necklace. It responds immediately with horrible creaking sounds and very slowly lifts its white arms which close in a perfect embrace around whatever happens to be next to it—in this case, a girl. The automaton holds her in its arms and now no one will be able to uncouple the living body from the body of iron, both equally beautiful. Suddenly the painted breasts of the Iron Maiden open, and five daggers appear that pierce her struggling companion whose hair is as long as its own.

Once the sacrifice is over another stone in the necklace is touched: the arms drop, the smile and the eyes fall shut, and the murderess becomes once again the Maiden, motionless in its coffin.

II. Death by Water

He is standing. And he is standing as
absolutely and definitely as if he were sitting.
WITOLD GOMBROWICZ

THE ROAD IS covered in snow and, inside the coach, the sombre lady wrapped in furs feels bored. Suddenly she calls out the name of one of the girls in her train. The girl is brought to her: the Countess bites her frantically and sticks needles in her flesh. A while later the procession abandons the wounded girl in the snow. The girl tries to run away. She is pursued, captured and pulled back into the coach. A little further along the road they halt: the Countess has ordered cold water. Now the girl is naked, standing in the snow. Night has fallen. A circle of torches surrounds her, held out by impassive footmen. They pour water over the body and the water turns to ice. (The Countess observes this from inside the coach.) The girl attempts one last slight gesture, trying to move closer to the torches—the only source of warmth. More water is poured over her, and there she remains, for ever standing, upright, dead.

III. The Lethal Cage

. . . scarlet and black wounds burst
upon the splendid flesh.
ARTHUR RIMBAUD

LINED WITH KNIVES and adorned with sharp iron blades, it can hold one human body, and can be lifted by means of a pulley. The ceremony of the cage takes place in this manner:

Dorko the maid drags in by the hair a naked young girl, shuts her up in the cage and lifts it high into the air. The Lady of These Ruins appears, a sleepwalker in white. Slowly and silently she sits upon a footstool placed underneath the contraption.

A red-hot poker in her hand, Dorko taunts the prisoner who, drawing back (and this is the ingenuity of the cage) stabs herself against the sharp irons while her blood falls upon the pale woman who dispassionately receives it, her eyes fixed on nothing, as in a daze. When the lady recovers from the trance, she slowly leaves the room. There have been two transformations: her white dress is now red, and where a girl once stood a corpse now lies.

IV. Classical Torture

Unblemished fruit, untouched by worm
or frost, whose firm, polished skin
cries out to be bitten!
BAUDELAIRE

EXCEPT FOR A few baroque refinements—like the Iron Maiden, death by water, or the cage—the Countess restricted herself to a monotonously classic style of torture that can be summed up as follows:

Several tall, beautiful, strong girls were selected—their ages had to be between 12 and 18—and dragged into the torture chamber where, dressed in white upon her throne, the countess awaited them. After binding their hands, the servants would whip the girls until the skin of their bodies ripped and they became a mass of swollen wounds; then the servants would burn them with red-hot pokers; cut their fingers with scissors or shears; pierce their wounds; stab them with daggers (if the Countess grew tired of hearing the cries they would sew their mouths up; if one of the girls fainted too soon they would revive her by burning paper soaked in oil between her legs). The blood spurted like fountains and the white dress of the nocturnal lady would turn red. So red, that she would have to go up to her room and change (what would she think about during this brief intermission?). The walls and the ceiling of the chamber would also turn red.

Not always would the lady remain idle while the others busied themselves around her. Sometimes she would lend a hand, and then, impetuously, tear at the flesh—in the most sensitive places—with tiny silver pincers; or she would stick needles, cut the skin between the fingers, press red-hot spoons and irons against the soles of the feet, use the whip (once, during one of her excursions, she ordered her servants to hold up a girl who had just died and kept on whipping her even though she was dead); she also murdered several by means of icy water (using a method invented by Darvulia, the witch; it consisted of plunging a girl into freezing water and leaving her there overnight). Finally, when she was sick, she would have the girls brought to her bedside and she would bite them.

During her erotic seizures she would hurl blasphemous insults at her victims. Blasphemous insults and cries like the baying of a she-wolf were her means of expression as she stalked, in a passion, the gloomy rooms. But nothing was more ghastly than her laugh. (I recapitulate: the medieval castle, the torture chamber, the tender young girls, the old and horrible servants, the beautiful madwoman laughing in a wicked ecstasy provoked by the suffering of others.) Her last words, before letting herself fall into a final faint, would be: "More, ever more, harder, harder!"

Not always was the day innocent, the night guilty. During the morning or the afternoon, young seamstresses would bring dresses for the Countess, and this would lead to innumerable scenes of cruelty. Without exception, Dorko would find mistakes in the sewing and would select two or three guilty victims (at this point the Countess's doleful eyes would glisten). The punishment of the seamstresses—and of the young maids in general—would vary. If the Countess happened to be in one of her rare good moods, Dorko would simply strip the victims who would continue to work, naked, under the Countess's eyes, in large rooms full of black cats. The girls bore this painless punishment in agonizing amazement, because they never believed it to be possible. Darkly, they must have felt terribly humiliated because their nakedness forced them into a kind of animal world, a feeling heightened by the fully clothed "human" presence of the Countess, watching them. This scene led me to think of

Death—Death as in old allegories, as in the Dance of Death. To strip naked is a prerogative of Death; another is the incessant watching over the creatures it has dispossessed. But there is more: sexual climax forces us into death-like gestures and expressions (gasping and writhing as in agony, cries and moans of paroxysm). If the sexual act implies a sort of death, Erzebet Bathory needed the visible, elementary, coarse death, to succeed in dying that other phantom death we call orgasm. But, who is Death? A figure that harrows and wastes wherever and however it pleases. This is also a possible description of the Countess Bathory. Never did anyone wish so hard not to grow old; I mean, to die. That is why, perhaps, she acted and played the role of Death. Because, how can Death possibly die?

Let us return to the seamstresses and the maids. If Erzebet woke up wrothful, she would not be satisfied with her *tableaux vivants*, but:

To the one who had stolen a coin she would repay with the same coin . . . red-hot, which the girl had to hold tight in her hand.

To the one who had talked during working hours, the Countess herself would sew her mouth shut, or otherwise would open her mouth and stretch it until the lips tore.

She also used the poker with which she would indiscriminately burn cheeks, breasts, tongues. . . .

When the punishments took place in Erzebet's chamber, at nighttime, it was necessary to spread large quantities of ashes around her bed, to allow the noble lady to cross without difficulties the vast pools of blood.

V. *On the Strength of a Name*

And cold madness wandered aimlessly
about the house.

MILOSZ

THE NAME OF Bathory—in the power of which Erzebet believed, as if it were an extraordinary talisman—was an illustrious one from the very early days of the Hungarian Empire. It was not by chance that the family coat-of-arms displayed the teeth of a wolf, because the Bathory were cruel, fearless and lustful. The many marriages that took place between blood relations contributed, perhaps, to the hereditary aberrations and diseases: epilepsy, gout, lust. It is not at all unlikely that Erzebet herself was an epileptic: she seemed possessed by seizures as unexpected as her terrible migraines and pains in the eyes (which she conjured away by placing a wounded pigeon, still alive, on her forehead).

The Countess's family was not unworthy of its ancestral fame. Her uncle Istvan, for instance, was so utterly mad that he would mistake summer for winter, and would have himself drawn in a sleigh along the burning sands that were, in his mind, roads covered with snow. Or consider her cousin Gabor, whose incestuous passion was reciprocated by his sister's. But the most charming of all was the celebrated aunt Klara. She had four husbands (the first two perished by her hand) and died a melodramatic death: she was caught in the arms of a casual acquaintance by her lover, a Turkish Pasha: the intruder was roasted on a spit and aunt Klara was raped (if this verb may be used in her respect) by the entire Turkish garrison. This however did not cause her death: on the contrary, her rapists—tired perhaps of having their way with her —finally had to stab her. She used to pick up her lovers along the Hungarian roads, and would not mind sprawling on a bed where she had previously slaughtered one of her female attendants.

By the time the Countess reached the age of forty, the Bathory had diminished or consumed themselves either through madness or through death. They became almost sensible, thereby losing the interest they had until then provoked in Erzebet.

VI. A Warrior Bridegroom

When the warrior took me in his arms
I felt the fire of pleasure . . .
THE ANGLO-SAXON ELEGY (VIII CEN.)

IN 1575, at the age of fifteen, Erzebet married Ferencz Nadasdy, a soldier of great courage. This simple soul never found out that the lady who inspired him with a certain love tinged by fear was in fact a monster. He would come to her in the brief respites between battles, drenched in horse-sweat and blood—the norms of hygiene had not yet been firmly established—and this probably stirred the emotions of the delicate Erzebet, always dressed in rich cloths and perfumed with costly scents.

One day, walking through the castle gardens, Nadasdy saw a naked girl tied to a tree. She was covered in honey: flies and ants crawled all over her, and she was sobbing. The Countess explained that the girl was purging the sin of having stolen some fruit. Nadasdy laughed candidly, as if she had told him a joke.

The soldier would not allow anyone to bother him with stories about his wife, stories of bites, needles, etc. A serious mistake: even as a newly-wed, during those crises whose formula was the Bathory's secret, Erzebet would prick her servants with long needles; and when, felled by her terrible migraines, she was forced to lie in bed, she would gnaw their shoulders and chew on the bits of flesh she had been able to extract. As if by magic, the girl's shrieks would soothe her pain.

But all this is child's play—a young girl's play. During her husband's life she never committed murder.

VII. The Melancholy Mirror

Everything is mirror!
OCTAVIO PAZ

THE COUNTESS WOULD spend her days in front of her large dark mirror; a famous mirror she had designed herself. It was so comfortable that it even had supports on which to lean one's arms, so as to be able to stand for many hours in front of it without feeling tired. We can suppose that while believing she had designed a mirror, Erzebet had in fact designed the plans for her lair. And now we can understand why only the most grippingly sad music of her gypsy orchestra, or dangerous hunting parties, or the violent perfume of the magic herbs in the witch's hut or—above all—the cellars flooded with human blood, could spark something resembling life in her perfect face. Because no one has more thirst for earth, for blood, and for ferocious sexuality than the creatures who inhabit cold mirrors. And on the subject of mirrors: the rumours concerning her alleged homosexuality were never confirmed. Was this allegation unconscious, or, on the contrary, did she accept it naturally, as simply another right to which she was entitled? Essentially she lived deep within an exclusively female world. There were only women during her nights of crime. And a few details are obviously revealing: for instance, in the torture chamber, during the moments of greatest tension, she herself used to plunge a burning candle into the sex of her victim. There are also testimonies which speak of less solitary pleasures. One of the servants said during the trial that an aristocratic and mysterious lady dressed as a young man would visit the Countess. On one occasion she saw them together, torturing a girl. But we do not know whether they shared any pleasures other than the sadistic ones.

More on the theme of the mirror: even though we are not concerned with *explaining* this sinister figure, it is necessary to dwell on the fact that she suffered from that sixteenth-century sickness: melancholia.

An unchangeable colour rules over the melancholic: his dwelling is a space the colour of mourning. Nothing happens in it. No one intrudes. It is a bare stage where the inert *I* is assisted by the *I* suffering from that inertia. The latter wishes to free the former, but all efforts fail, as Theseus would have failed had he been not only himself, but also the Minotaur; to kill him then, he would have had to kill himself. But there are fleeting remedies: sexual pleasures, for instance, can, for a brief moment, obliterate the silent gallery of echoes and mirrors that constitutes the melancholic soul. Even more: they can illuminate the funeral chamber and transform it into a sort of musical box with gaily-coloured figurines that sing and dance deliciously. Afterwards, when the music winds down, the soul will return to immobility and silence. The music box is not a gratuitous comparison. Melancholia is, I believe, a musical problem: a dissonance, a change in rhythm. While on the *outside* everything happens with the vertiginous rhythm of a cataract, on the *inside* is the exhausted *adagio* of drops of water falling from time to tired time. For this reason the *outside*, seen from the melancholic *inside*, appears absurd and unreal, and constitutes "the farce we must all play." But for an instant—because of a wild music, or a drug, or the sexual act carried to its climax—the very slow rhythm of the melancholic soul does not only rise to that of the outside world: it overtakes it with an ineffably blissful exorbitance, and the soul then thrills animated by delirious new energies.

The melancholic soul sees Time as suspended before and after the fatally ephemeral violence. And yet the truth is that time is never suspended, but it grows as slowly as the fingernails of the dead. Between two silences or two deaths, the prodigious, brief moment of speed takes on the various forms of lust: from an innocent intoxication to sexual perversions and even murder.

I think of Erzebet Bathory and her nights whose rhythms are measured by the cries of adolescent girls. I see a portrait of the Countess: the sombre and beautiful lady resembles the allegories of Melancholia represented in old engravings. I also recall that in her time, a melancholic person was a person possessed by the Devil.

VIII. Black Magic

. . . who kills the sun in order to install
the reign of darkest night.
ANTONIN ARTAUD

ERZEBET'S GREATEST OBSESSION had always been to keep old age at bay, at any cost. Her total devotion to the arts of black magic was aimed at preserving—intact for all eternity—the "sweet bird" of her youth. The magical herbs, the incantations, the amulets, even the blood baths had, in her eyes, a medicinal function: to immobilize her beauty in order to become, for ever and ever, *a dream of stone*. She always lived surrounded by talismans. In her years of crime she chose one single talisman which contained an ancient and filthy parchment on which was written in special ink, a prayer for her own personal use. She carried it close to her heart, underneath her costly dresses, and in the midst of a celebration, she would touch it surreptitiously. I translate the prayer:

> Help me, oh Isten; and you also, all-powerful
> cloud. Protect me, Erzebet, and grant me long life.
> Oh cloud, I am in danger. Send me ninety cats, for
> you are the supreme mistress of cats. Order them to
> assemble here from all their dwelling-places: from
> the mountains, from the waters, from the rivers,
> from the gutters and from the oceans. Tell them to
> come quickly and bite the heart of ——— and also
> the heart of ——— and of ———. And to also bite
> and rip the heart of Megyery, the Red. And keep
> Erzebet from all evil.

The blanks were to be filled with the names of those whose hearts she wanted bitten.

In 1604 Erzebet became a widow and met Darvulia. Darvulia was exactly like the woodland witch who frightens us in children's tales. Very old, irascible, always surrounded by black cats, Darvulia fully responded to Erzebet's fascination: within the Countess's eyes the witch found a new version of the evil powers buried in the poisons of the forest and in the coldness of the moon. Darvulia's black magic wrought itself in the Countess's black silence. She initiated her to even crueller games; she taught her to look upon death, and the *meaning* of looking upon death. She incited her to seek death and blood in a literal sense: that is, to love them for their own sake, without fear.

IX. Blood Baths

If you go bathing, Juanilla,
tell me to what baths you go.
CANCIONERO OF UPSALA

THIS RUMOUR EXISTED: since the arrival of Darvulia, the Countess, in order to preserve her comeliness, took baths of human blood. True: Darvulia, being a witch, believed in the invigorating powers of the "human fluid." She proclaimed the merits of young girls' blood—especially if they were virgins—to vanquish the demon of senility, and the Countess accepted the treatment as meekly as if it had been a salt bath. Therefore, in the torture chamber, Dorko applied herself to slicing veins and arteries; the blood was collected in pitchers and, when the victims were bled dry, Dorko would pour the red warm liquid over the body of the waiting Countess—ever so quiet, ever so white, ever so erect, ever so silent.

In spite of her unchangeable beauty, Time inflicted upon her some of the vulgar signs of its passing. Towards 1610 Darvulia mysteriously disappeared and Erzebet, almost fifty, complained to her new witch about the uselessness of the blood baths. In fact, more than complain, she threatened to kill her if she did not stop at once the encroaching and execrable signs of old age. The witch argued that Darvulia's method had not worked because plebeian blood had been used. She assured—or prophesied—that changing the colour of the blood, using blue blood instead of red, would ensure the fast retreat of old age. Here began the hunt for the daughters of gentlemen. To attract them, Erzebet's minions would argue that the Lady of Csejthe, alone in her lonely castle, could not resign herself to her solitude. And how to banish solitude? Filling the dark halls with young girls of good families who, in exchange for happy company, would receive lessons in fine manners and learn how to behave exquisitely in society. A fortnight later, of the twenty-five "pupils" who had hurried to become aristocrats, only two were left: one died some time later, bled white; the other managed to take her life.

X. *The Castle of Csejthe*

The stone walk is paved with dark cries.
PIERRE-JEAN JOUVE

A CASTLE OF grey stones, few windows, square towers, underground mazes; a castle high upon a cliff, a hillside of dry windblown weeds, of woods full of white beasts in winter and dark beasts in summer; a castle that Erzebet Bathory loved for the doleful silence of its walls which muffled every cry.

The Countess's room, cold and badly lit by a lamp of jasmine oil, reeked of blood, and the cellars reeked of dead bodies. Had she wanted to, she could have carried out her work in broad daylight and murdered the girls under the sun, but she was fascinated by the gloom of her dungeon. The gloom which matched so keenly her terrible eroticism of stone, snow and walls. She loved her maze-shaped dungeon, the archetypical hell of our fears; the viscous, insecure space where we are unprotected and can get lost.

What did she do with all of her days and nights, there, in the loneliness of Csejthe? Of her nights we know something. During the day, the Countess would not leave the side of her two old servants, two creatures escaped from a painting by Goya: the dirty, malodorous, incredibly ugly and perverse Dorko and Jo Ilona. They would try to amuse her with domestic tales to which she paid no attention, and yet she needed the continuous and abominable chatter. Another way of passing time was to contemplate her jewels, to look at herself in her famous mirror, to change her dresses fifteen times a day. Gifted with a great practical sense, she saw to it that the underground cellars were always well supplied; she also concerned herself with her daughters' future—her daughters who always lived so far away from her; she administered her fortune with intelligence, and she occupied herself with all the little details that rule the profane order of our lives.

XI. Severe Measures

... the law, cold and aloof by its very nature,
has no access to the passions that might
justify the cruel act of murder.
SADE

FOR SIX YEARS the Countess murdered with impunity. During those years there had been countless rumours about her. But the name of Bathory, not only illustrious but also diligently protected by the Hapsburgs, frightened her possible accusers.

Towards 1610 the king had in his hands the most sinister reports—together with proofs—concerning the Countess. After much hesitation he decided to act. He ordered the powerful Thurzo, Count Palatine, to investigate the tragic events at Csejthe and to punish the guilty parties.

At the head of a contingent of armed men, Thurzo arrived unannounced at the castle. In the cellar, cluttered with the remains of the previous night's bloody ceremony, he found a beautiful mangled corpse and two young girls who lay dying. But that was not all. He smelt the smell of the dead; he saw the walls splattered with blood; he saw the Iron Maiden, the cage, the instruments of torture, bowls of dried blood, the cells—and in one of them a group of girls who were waiting their turn to die and who told him that after many days of fasting they had been served roast flesh that had once belonged to the bodies of their companions.

The Countess, without denying Thurzo's accusations, declared that these acts were all within her rights as a noble woman of ancient lineage. To which the Count Palatine replied: "Countess, I condemn you to life imprisonment within your castle walls."

Deep in his heart, Thurzo must have told himself that the Countess should be beheaded, but such an exemplary punishment would have been frowned upon, because it affected not only the Bathory family, but also the nobility in general. In the meantime, a notebook was found in the Countess's room, filled with the names and descriptions of her 610 victims in her handwriting. The followers of Erzebet, when brought before the judge, confessed to unthinkable deeds, and perished on the stake.

Around her the prison grew. The doors and windows of her room were walled up; only a small opening was left in one of the walls to allow her to receive her food. And when everything was ready, four gallows were erected on the four corners of the castle to indicate that within those walls lived a creature condemned to death.

In this way she lived for three years, almost wasting away with cold and hunger. She never showed the slightest sign of repentance. She never understood why she had been condemned. On August 21, 1614, a contemporary historian wrote: "She died at dawn, abandoned by everyone."

She was never afraid, she never trembled. And no compassion, no sympathy or admiration may be felt for her. Only a certain astonishment at the enormity of the horror, a fascination with a white dress that turns red, with the idea of total laceration, with the imagination of a silence starred with cries in which everything reflects an unacceptable beauty.

Like Sade in his writings, and Gilles de Rais in his crimes, the Countess Bathory reached beyond all limits the uttermost pit of unfettered passions. She is yet another proof that the absolute freedom of the human creature is horrible.

Translated by Alberto Manguel

Man's Dwelling Place

ANGÉLICA GORODISCHER

SCIENCE FICTION IS not popular among writers in either Portuguese or Spanish. In Argentina, however, one publishing company, Sudamericana, under the direction of Francisco Porrúa, began publishing the Anglo-Saxon classics of the genre, and this inspired a few writers to try their hand at the game. Among the brave pioneers were Alberto Vanasco; Hector G. Oesterheld, whose comic strip El eternauta ("The Infinity-Traveler") became a hallowed classic; Eduardo Goligorski; Marie Langer; and especially, Angélica Gorodischer. In 1964 she won a short-story competition: this encouraged her to continue writing, and Opus dos (Opus Two) was published as part of the Minotauro series three years later. Critics have compared her work to that of Philip José Farmer; she prefers to acknowledge the influence of Philip K. Dick, Ursula K. Le Guin, and Anne McCaffrey, as well as "the distant shades of Lord Dunsany and Jan Potocki."

> So He drove out the man; and He placed
> at the East of the Garden of Eden Cherubims,
> and a flaming sword which turned every way,
> to keep the way of the tree of life.
> GENESIS 3:24

WE ENTERED THE city at 8:30 A.M. local time. I must bring to Your Lordship's attention the fact that the members of the crew under my command seemed uneasy, almost frightened. At the time I attributed their condition to the peace and quiet —I don't think I was mistaken. It was a clear day, the weather was mild, and the sun, the breeze and the grasshoppers made us think of a fairly advanced spring. Our heavy clothing bothered us, leather hems dug into our flesh and I'm certain that all of us would have preferred to wear the sandals we kept on board ship and not the regulation disembarkment boots. The streets were lined with fruit-laden trees, fruit that looked still green, a whitish or yellowish green, cold, but which seemed to mellow, turn golden, before our very eyes. In the official report I have detailed the itinerary we followed. Your Lordship will find marked in red upon the map hereby enclosed, the various houses we entered. They were all uninhabited. Furnished, ready to be lived in, with flowers in vases, breakfasts on the tables, curtains floating in the breeze—but empty. They all looked clean and fresh, their windows open onto the green gardens—but empty. The streets were also empty. In the official report I have tried to be as objective as possible, as if this mission were no different from any of the previous ones. But here I wish to give Your Lordship some idea of what we felt, the crew and myself, as we entered the empty city; and later, when we saw the city's inhabitants. I don't think I know how to use emotional language, so I must return again and again to the clinical description of what we saw. Your Lordship will excuse the repetitions, which are perhaps useless. Leaving the sixth house (in which we had seen camp-beds, mirrors, a round wooden table with a yellow tablecloth, white cups, a bird in a cage, recently-watered plants, an open awning over a deck) one of the men suggested we turn back. I didn't consider his suggestion a breach of discipline; I put my right hand on the butt of my gun (my gun is always unloaded; I have never fired against anyone and I would not have fired against him, but I could have arrested him and left him in solitary confinement on board ship) and told him to stay exactly where he was, while I and the others carried on into the heart of the city. I do not know what my men were thinking; I could sense their fear but not read their thoughts. For my part, I could not stop remembering our grey cities, the factory chimneys, the slums, the lack of trees and green places, the metallic smells, the skyscrapers, the windy corners on cold afternoons, the mad traffic, the dirt, the noise. Here was a happy, golden city, golden and green, green and peaceful. Its inhabitants had just died, or were invisible. But I wished I could have been born here, grow up here, live and die in a city like this. There were no cars, the roads were softly curved, the streets were not really streets: they were walks, country walks through gardens; the houses were low and white, one for each family, with a fenceless yard, with trees. There were no tall buildings, no commercial or industrial areas, no civic centres, no temples. As soon as I realized that the whole city had been built as a home, a place to live in, I stopped being afraid. I confess, Your Lordship, after so many years, that I have felt fear several times, but I have always been able to free myself from fear through sheer willpower. But not this time. Fear had gripped hold of me from the moment I realized (thinking it was true) that the city was uninhabited but alive; and then fear left me, without even having to think about it, helplessly. It left me when I felt that here at last was man's dwelling-place, and I longed to sit on the ground in the shadow of a large tree, then enter one of the houses, eat the hurried, voracious breakfast of youth, lie on one of the beds full of the nodding weariness of old age. I thought of nests, hide-aways, caves, sailing ships, apartment houses, carpeted offices, clandestine brothels, all that man has invented to protect himself from the outside world, to hide himself from the eyes of others, to exorcise his miseries, to try and prove that he is alive—and the thought somehow explained the disappearance of my fear. At this point I wish to inform Your Lordship of what we learnt later from the inhabitants of the city. (This has been explained in more technical terms in the report drafted by the mission's engineer who made a careful study of the structures.) The houses had been functioning on their own for a very long time—for many years, many generations. Their mechanisms keep them alive, clean them, close the windows when it rains, light the fires when it is cold, change the bed linen, dish out the breakfasts and lunches, prepare fresh lemonade in summer and rum-punch in winter. But we, who do not have living houses, houses with hands and brains, imagined that their inhabitants had just abandoned them. At last we reached the central square. I call it "square" (as I did in the report) in the hope of making myself understood. It was not a dry stone square with cement borders and monuments and shrivelled moss sprouting from its cracks; neither was it a park with flower-beds and rose-bushes and pergolas. It was the land, I imagine, man discovered when he stopped being a nomad and a hunter; when he stopped in his tracks and instead of pitching a tent, built a house; when he harnessed his horse to a plough instead of holding it ready to ride away. It was a rippling field surrounded by the city, green, with trees and a very narrow river. The inhabitants of the city were there. They lay on the green, eyes wide open, their hair mingling with the grass. And the breeze blew their clothing, the breeze moved through the trees and lifted their tunics, making their ribbons and tresses float in the air. They were not dead, they were breathing. We walked among them, we called to them, we bent over them shading their open eyes from the sun, trying to make them see us. Your Lordship has read the report, so I will not repeat myself. I will not describe yet again our efforts to communicate with them, nor the ritual of sounds and gestures that some of them performed before speaking to us. I remember I leaned over a cross-eyed woman who was telling me about their waiting, while a few of my men, on their hands and knees, were calling me over to the bodies lying face upwards, to listen to the words of the citizens of the golden city I now longed for, had always longed for, had ventured through to reach these immortal chrysalids. I told my men to write everything down, carefully, and then settled down to listen, but the woman was no longer talking. I had to start again, this time with a young boy who could have been my son, even my grandson, and for whom I felt not pity but violent envious hatred. The cross-eyed woman had opened her mouth and shut it again, like a fish, seven times, and had waited for a cloud to pass over a tree behind her head, and had blown her breath into my face: that was the only way, she later said, for her to be able to speak to a stranger. Had she wanted to speak to one of the other creatures lying there, the series of signs, signals and sounds would have been different, and she would have had to wait in turn, before receiving an answer, for the chain of seemingly senseless codes that the unlimited space had prompted them to invent. With the young boy I was more patient and less afraid. His rhythm of life depended on the signals he received, but he constantly doubted the meaning of these signals, and speaking to me caused him such unease that in the end he sank deeply into a kind of coma. He never spoke to the others, but I was something so out of the ordinary, that he felt he could wager with a large margin

of certainty on the possibility of my being, I myself, a favour-
able omen. The signs and messages reached him both from
the outside world and from within himself; and for him, the
first interpretation he made of them was the only valid and
true one. But then a second meaning formed itself in his
mind, a meaning that might be either a deceitful version, or
the true one, hidden and delayed by the first. Because of this
doubt he would hesitate to believe his first interpretation. All
this would condition all future actions—actions never to be
carried out—because he kept looking for new facts to confirm
and help interpret all the previously acquired information. I
left him and ordered our retreat after checking to see what
our crew had been able to obtain. I felt a growing hostility
towards these quiet people, and I also felt furious with myself
because of my inefficiency. I kept telling myself I should have
stopped here to find at least one who would stand out among
the young motionless bodies, their beautiful open eyes, the
floating gauze, the fallen hands. Now I realize that I was
looking for an image of Your Lordship: a leader, a wise old
man, a commander of the people. But there was none, and I
ask myself: had there been one, would they all have lain down
there to live mingled with the grass, one with the earth, deep
in their own unchangeable belief, each waiting calmly for
death, looked after by the electronic houses, nourished,
dressed, fertilized, combed, perfumed, shod by cybernetic
constructions guarded by their own cyclops' nests? The answer is yes, and Your Lordship will now understand the conclusions of my report. I believe that we, the descendants of
those who left our planet convinced of its destruction, should
not return home. It is true: mankind did not destroy itself. It
reached happiness, balance, perfection. Mankind built
golden cities on which they bestowed hands and eyes, elimi-
nating, as worthless, work and money. But we, who live in
murky towns of constant turmoil, we who travel and toil and

make love and commit suicide and betray each other and drive noisy, dangerous vehicles, we, the younger brothers of Man, should not return. For us Paradise is irretrievably lost, and it is better that way: now we belong only to ourselves. I, a pacifist, a disciple of Your Lordship, a speaker for nonviolence, am here defending war, killings, tortures. I say that I myself will kill, fire guns, drop bombs, destroy and torture, if thereby I will avoid lying on the grass waiting for death, unravelling a useless ritual that will not even allow me to know whether I am alive or dead, permitting myself to be dressed, washed, combed, my semen extracted to fertilize women I cannot see, protected from the rain, fed, looked after. My opinion—even though I remember with pain the golden, motionless, empty city—is that the results of this expedition to the third planet from the Sun should not be made public. I cannot end this personal letter to Your Lordship without mentioning that the city had a name full of promise, transparent and lofty, that does not appear in the official report, and that the mothering river that crossed the garden looked as silver-plated as its name, beneath the midday sun, the day we left.

Translated by Alberto Manguel

Knight, Death and the Devil

VLADY KOCIANCICH

In 1967 I was asked to set up a series of anthologies for a small Argentine publishing company. It occurred to me that it would be interesting to choose one subject—a newspaper clipping, a painting, the possible first sentence of a story— and ask a number of writers to compose their own versions of this subject. We called the series Variations and for the second volume used Dürer's engraving Knight, Death and the Devil *as the given theme. Jorge Luis Borges (who contributed a couple of sonnets to the volume) suggested we include the work of one of his students, Vlady Kociancich. We agreed, and the following story was later included in Kociancich's first collection,* Coraje (Courage). *Since then she has published several other books, notably* La octava maravilla (The Eighth Wonder), *a remarkable novel that received critical acclaim both in Spain and in Argentina.*

A Gentle Knight was pricking on the plaine,
Y cladd in mightie armes and siluer shielde. . . .
. . . on his brest a bloudie Crosse he bore,
the deare remembrance of his dying Lord. . . .

SPENSER, *THE FAERIE QUEENE*

I STOPPED AT THE first turning of the path that crossed the forest. The moon, after shredding its way through the tree-tops, appeared suddenly full, above my head, violently illuminating my coat of armour, turning me into the ghost of a knight whose only real features were his weariness and low spirits. Even in the dim light that came from the heavens my eyes were burning. I did not allow myself the time to dwell on the annoying sweat crawling, multiplying itself along my body, beneath the weight of my armour, down the barely curved line of my back. I remembered the long day in the sun and, as all men have done sometime, I blessed the darkness and the night. I was riding towards my father's castle. Something stronger than impatience, perhaps the delight of a return so long desired, made me loiter foolishly on the road to admire a tree carved with my initials, to discover in the hieroglyphics of its branches and leaves the lost steps of my childhood. I was in no hurry, and as I basked in the calm of knowing myself home again, night came upon me.

When a boy casts aside the sweet protection of the walls which surround his birthplace, and steers away from the familiar voices and faces to test his mettle in war, to leave his blood on foreign ground or to return victorious, then that boy becomes a man. And when the man returns not knowing well what it is he has won in the Name of the Lord, what it is that weighs so heavily on his soul, that man wants once again to be the boy he was. These were my thoughts, when my horse's hooves no longer sounded muffled on the soft earth and made instead a hollow, metallic sound. Water. A barely moving thread of water, more mud than anything else. I halted and looked carefully around me. At night the world does not seem the same, but even though I could not see more than the narrow strip of road, I knew they were waiting for me. I pulled the reins and led my horse towards where I felt the meeting would take place. Until the moment of entering the clearing I doubted its very existence. The moon had faded the greenery and the delicate web of forest flowers. This was a silver field inside the forest, and in the middle of the field was yet another circle of light that seemed to spring mysteriously from the ground. I dismounted and stared at the pond while a nostalgic yearning grew voluptuously inside me. I took off my helmet and touched for the first time my sweat-sodden head. With difficulty I knelt among the reeds which broke without a sound, and I wet my face. Fresh water, crystal-clear, pure, innocent water. An idea more dangerous than sin, the heretic conviction that Nature is innocent, suddenly took hold of me. Patiently (there was no other way) I lifted off my armour. It was a bothersome and ridiculous task because there was no one there to help me, and the heat that had built up during the day stifled me. Before entering the water I intended to ask God His forgiveness for this fault and for the risk I was taking, promising that I would pay for it by increasing the ranks of the enemies of Christ in the underground army of Satan, but I decided not to compound my sin by adding to it a blasphemy. In the water, the shirt I had kept on hindered my swimming, so I took it off and threw it onto the shore. Now I could enjoy myself with no cares, diving in, stretching full length, turning around in the coolness of the pond that had known me as a boy and now received me as man, a man victorious and a transgressor beyond repentance. As I came out of the water, naked, throwing my hair back and drying it with my hands, a vague unease came over me. I dressed myself, feeling ashamed, beneath the moon, very clumsily because my happiness had made me tired. I was about to climb back onto my horse when I felt my right hand touch a skin, a serpentine dampness. Before seeing what I was to see, I realized two things: that it was dark and that I was alone. I could not scream even though fear or surprise rose to my throat. The creature looked like several things at once, and yet fully like none, creatures that seemed even more horrible because they were common, familiar beasts: a wolf, a goat, a serpent. Disproportionate, absurd, his laugh was the laugh of a man. I saw him lean towards me, I smelt the stench Our Lord has marked him with to warn us and which I was now to recognize even in my dreams—that is, if what was happening to me was not itself a dream. With a hand which I was not able to close completely I clutched at my sword and lifted the cross-shaped hilt in front of the Devil's mad eyes. He neither backed away nor drew nearer. In the tortuous silence of nightmares, I mounted my horse. The Devil was not coming after me, but I could sense him growing vaster in the shadows.

It took me a great effort to calm down. I was still trembling, shamelessly—because the fear of the unknown does not taint a man's courage—when I saw, as a bird sees his nest, the powerful bastions of my home, taller than the tallest branches in the wood, appearing and disappearing before my eyes at every turn of the road. Now it was as if nothing had happened. There was my home, my family expecting me, my mother, my proud father, and my friend Guy, the Frenchman, younger than I and still learning the art of battle. Nothing had taken place. Neither the beautiful war nor the miseries of war, neither the splendours of the sea nor the misfortunes of travel. I no longer remembered my brave comrades, the pure, the strong, the sometimes hateful soldiers of God. Neither did I remember the doubts I had felt. Only in the moment of triumph or in the heat of the battle half lost or half won, had I felt towards these comrades a brotherly love. The rest of the time, during the long pauses that opened my eyes to the corruption and deceit, to the horrible discoveries of rape, starving children, mutilated bodies, I had been separated from the others. Between the ruin and the plunder of victory, my thoughts had drawn me apart, made me resentful. One single thought had torn me away from my doubts and allowed me to carry on: the certainty of fighting for the right cause, with no other purpose than that of defending what was best in this world, in spite of mankind and of myself.

The German knights took exception to my friend Guy. They said that he was closer to Hell than to salvation, closer to the everlasting fire than to Paradise, a foreigner who had not yet been ordained and who did not belong to any known brotherhood in his homeland. But what did they know of Guy? Perhaps it was his lax chastity which allowed him to be humble and generous with the weak. Intelligent, brave, deft with his sword—my friend Guy. Next time we would ride together.

When I reached the castle's drawbridge I could think of nothing except my distant and perfect past, the marvellous days without doubts or responsibilities, almost without sorrows. I spurred my horse to cross the bridge when a troubling thought crossed my mind. The bridge had been lowered. Why? There were no guards about. The habit of war made me stop and look cautiously around. Then suddenly, in the moonlight, on that both brilliant and cloudy night, a figure ran towards me. My hand, not I, gripped my sword. But it was only a woman: I heard her laughter.

We met in the middle of the bridge. She was dancing. She moved her arms around madly, first to the left, then to the right, her skirts flying about in a sudden gust of wind. I stared at her curiously, not knowing what to do or what to say. The plump dancing body barred my way: a peasant-woman, her eyes wide open, as if she were listening carefully, her laughter shrill and vulgar. I asked her:

"Is there a feast at the castle?"

She lifted her face towards me, but neither answered nor stopped dancing.

I saw her stretch a trembling hand towards the reins, but I did nothing to stop her. "Perhaps," I thought, "all this is part of a new game, a ceremony," and I allowed her to lead the horse towards the gateway.

"Woman, do you know who I am?"

Without a word, without stopping her dance, she led me on. As soon as we crossed the bridge, I noticed the glimmer of a fire in the dark.

"So there is a feast!" I shouted.

The peasant-woman laughed convulsively, pointing a finger at me as if she were accusing me in front of nobody, and then she left me, dancing and shaking and finally disappearing down an ill-lit corridor.

I would have followed her, but a cry made me turn my head towards the fire. A group of men and women formed a haphazard circle around the crackling flames. Missing something I could not well define, perhaps the customary etiquette, I drew near them. On the bonfire—I could now see it was a bonfire—a body was writhing in pain. Terrified and unable to believe my eyes, covering my nose and mouth with my hands, I drew nearer. Among billows of smoke and disfigured by the torture, I recognized the face of my friend Guy. I wanted to throw myself on the flames to free him, but countless arms held me back.

"Guy, Guy!" I cried. "What have they done to you?"

The eyes of the dying boy opened to stare at me.

"Hermann. . . ."

The beloved face grimaced and managed to smile a familiar

smile, fighting the pain. I made out his words perfectly, in spite of the clamour and my own cries.

"It is nothing . . . ," he said.

Even my despair was insufficient to fight the weight of the crowd that made my metal prison even heavier. When they let go of me it was too late. Guy had become one single flame.

They drew me away from him firmly, respectfully explaining something I failed to understand. In between fits of coughing and of nausea, I allowed them to take off my armour, I allowed solicitous and repugnant hands to dress me in a silken shirt, a velvet jacket, a cape. Astounded and horrified, I let them lead me up to the room where my parents were resting. I advanced among people I did not know and who contaminated the painful welcoming ceremony. I no longer heard the voices that kept on explaining; only the voice of my friend Guy: "Hermann, it is nothing. . . ." Neither did I notice the upheaval along the corridors and hallways, the absence of the usual servants, the presence of a disorderly and mixed crowd. They opened the door that separated me from my mother, and in a daze, I looked for her. She was next to the bed of my father who seemed asleep. I reached out for her and she turned her face towards my voice. Her pale face grew paler.

"Mother, it is I."

She answered in a tone I had never heard before.

"Go away, Hermann, go away! Oh, why did you have to come back now?"

"What has happened? I've seen Guy. . . ."

"They found him guilty of the plague."

I understood that my father was dead and that Guy had been condemned by the terror. I learnt that my mother would die and that I would die as well. I caught her in my arms as she fainted. I lay her next to my father as if she were sleeping.

Later I walked down the deserted hallways. Sometimes the

remains of polite manners in the midst of the panic would make a head bow in homage as it recognized me, and then drift away. I wished for war, for the clean death on the battle-field. I wished for a visible enemy who would lend worth to this body already condemned, to this other armour. I wished not to be where I was: unable to do anything, barely witnessing the end of all I had loved.

In the courtyard I saw Guy's body burn. The pile of corpses was growing. I fetched my horse and mounted. I did not want to escape, I simply wanted to leave. It made me despair not to understand the stupid death of those for whom I had fought in the East, fought to honour them with my own honour and with the clear proof of my courage. A dog ran after me, whining. But I was not alone. I carried the mourn-ful following of my lost family, of Guy's useless torture—Guy whom I knew to be innocent. I carried the denied embrace of my mother, the false sleep of my father, my absent or dead cousins.

During that long and splendid summer's morning I rode in circles followed by my dog and by the painful memory of what had happened. That afternoon I let myself fall on the harsh ground in the woods, without the strength to eat or sleep. Human vanities never seem as vain as when we are about to lose them—so precious, so fragile, so incomprehensible. Night fell without my realizing it. Stretched out on the ground I could see my friend Guy's eyes, and hear his voice again: "Hermann, it is nothing. . . ." Again I would see my mother's pale face among the shadows, and the Duke's body seemed to decompose by my side. All night long I watched alone over my dead, waiting for my death and for the death of my dog who at length had fallen asleep. Dawn came as quickly as the night that had passed.

And I was not dead. My skin felt clean, my face refreshed. God had spared my life. In despair, in anger, I cried, still surrounded by the bleak circle of my people. The pride of pain made me stand up with a cry, and clench a fist at heaven on this morning so radiant it seemed the very first morning of the world.

"If you have not forgotten me, I want a proof," I shouted. "I have no reason to live. I need something to believe in, other than this senseless destruction, these useless horrors, this emptiness."

I said no more; even the birds were silent. Not a sound, not a leaf rustling in the wind. I walked aimlessly towards my horse. The dog shook itself and trotted happily after me.

Once mounted, I suddenly noticed that I was in the same clearing of the woods where I had stopped two nights ago. Next to the edge of the water were two figures. One was the Devil. The other was inconceivable Death, the dirty, bedraggled death of the flesh, smiling at me with a lipless smile, staring at me without eyes, spurring its horse in my direction. I looked around me. My mother, my father, Guy were no longer there.

I thanked my compassionate God, my generous God. I did what I was supposed to do. Accompanied by my dog, by the Devil, by Death, I turned back towards my castle. We crossed the bridge and I placed myself at the head of a group of fleeing peasants laden with parcels, men and women who had abandoned their children, their parents, their brothers and sisters. I said to them:

"I am your master, the Duke."

I gave the order and the bridge was raised.

Translated by Alberto Manguel

The Shunammite

INÉS ARREDONDO

UNLIKE THE VAST majority of Mexican writing, which is deeply rooted in historical events, the stories of Inés Arredondo do not belong to one specific moment in history. They bring to life archetypal female figures—Eve, Jocasta, Medea, the Shunammite—seen from inside the women themselves. "Eve was framed," which has now become a feminist slogan, was used by Arredondo in 1965 in her first collection of stories, La señal (The Sign). Arrendondo's stories have only one setting: the north coast of the San Lorenzo River, not far from the sea. This area has become hers in the sense that Nottinghamshire belongs to D. H. Lawrence, a writer whose influence she acknowledges. In this flat, open space, Arrendondo's women seek to define themselves, destroying the traditional interpretation of their character. In Arredondo's telling, King David's "young virgin," the Shunammite, becomes the sacrificial victim of a male-dominated society.

> So they sought for a fair damsel throughout all
> the coasts of Israel, and found Abishag, a
> Shunammite, and brought her to the king. . . .
>
> And the damsel was very fair, and
> cherished the king, and ministered to him;
> but the king knew her not.
> KINGS I: 1, 3–4

THE SUMMER HAD been a fiery furnace. The last summer of my youth.

Tense, concentrated in the arrogance that precedes combustion, the city shone in a dry and dazzling light. I stood in the very midst of the light, dressed in mourning, proud, feeding the flames with my blonde hair, alone. Men's sly glances slid over my body without soiling it, and my haughty modesty forced them to barely nod at me, full of respect. I was certain of having the power to dominate passions, to purify anything in the scorching air that surrounded but did not singe me.

Nothing changed when I received the telegram; the sadness it brought me did not affect in the least my feelings towards the world. My uncle Apolonio was dying at the age of seventy-odd years and wanted to see me. I had lived as a daughter in his house for many years and I sincerely felt pain at the thought of his inevitable death. All this was perfectly normal, and not a single omen, not a single shiver made me suspect anything. Quickly I made arrangements for the journey, in the very same untouchable midst of the motionless summer.

I arrived at the village during the hour of siesta.

Walking down the empty streets with my small suitcase, I fell to daydreaming, in that dusky zone between reality and time, born of the excessive heat. I was not remembering; I was almost reliving things as they had been. "Look, Licha, the *amapas* are blooming again." The clear voice, almost childish. "I want you to get yourself a dress like that of Margarita Ibarra to wear on the sixteenth." I could hear her, feel her walking by my side, her shoulders bent a little forwards, light in spite of her plumpness, happy and old. I carried on walking in the company of my aunt Panchita, my mother's sister. "Well, my dear, if you *really* don't like Pepe . . . but he's such a *nice* boy. . . ." Yes, she had used those exact words, here, in front of Tichi Valenzuela's window, with her gay smile, innocent and impish. I walked a little further, where the paving stones seemed to fade away in the haze, and when the bells rang, heavy and real, ending the siesta and announcing the Rosary, I opened my eyes and gave the village a good, long look: it was not the same. The *amapas* had not bloomed and I was crying, in my mourning dress, at the door of my uncle's house.

The front gate was open, as always, and at the end of the courtyard rose the bougainvillea. As always: but not the same. I dried my tears, and felt that I was not arriving: I was leaving. Everything looked motionless, pinioned in my memory, and the heat and the silence seemed to wither it all. My footsteps echoed with a new sound, and Maria came out to greet me.

"Why didn't you let us know? We'd have sent . . ."

We went straight into the sick man's room. As I entered, I felt cold. Silence and gloom preceded death.

"Luisa, is that you?"

The dear voice was dying out and would soon be silent for ever.

"I'm here, uncle."

"God be praised! I won't die alone."

"Don't say that; you'll soon be much better."

He smiled sadly; he knew I was lying but he did not want to make me cry.

"Yes, my daughter. Yes. Now have a rest, make yourself at home and then come and keep me company. I'll try to sleep a little."

Shrivelled, wizened, toothless, lost in the immense bed and floating senselessly in whatever was left of his life, he was painful to be with, like something superfluous, out of place, like so many others at the point of death. Stepping out of the overheated passageway, one would take a deep breath, instinctively, hungry for light and air.

I began to nurse him and I felt happy doing it. This house was *my* house, and in the morning, while tidying up, I would sing long-forgotten songs. The peace that surrounded me came perhaps from the fact that my uncle no longer awaited death as something imminent and terrible, but instead let himself be carried by the passing days towards a more or less distant or nearby future, with the unconscious tenderness of a child. He would go over his past life with great pleasure and enjoy imagining that he was bequeathing me his images, as grandparents do with their children.

"Bring me that small chest, there, in the large wardrobe. Yes, that one. The key is underneath the mat, next to Saint Anthony. Bring the key as well."

And his sunken eyes would shine once again at the sight of all his treasures.

"Look: this necklace—I gave it to your aunt for our tenth wedding anniversary. I bought it in Mazatlan from a Polish jeweller who told me God-knows-what story about an Austrian princess, and asked an impossible price for it. I brought it back hidden in my pistol-holder and didn't sleep a wink in the stagecoach—I was so afraid someone would steal it!"

The light of dusk made the young, living stones glitter in his callused hands.

". . . this ring, so old, belonged to my mother; look carefully at the miniature in the other room and you'll see her wearing it. Cousin Begona would mutter behind her back that a sweetheart of hers . . ."

The ladies in the portraits would move their lips and speak, once again, would breathe again—all these ladies he had seen, he had touched. I would picture them in my mind and understand the meaning of these jewels.

"Have I told you about the time we travelled to Europe, in 1908, before the Revolution? You had to take a ship to Colima. . . . And in Venice your aunt Panchita fell in love with a certain pair of ear-rings. They were much too expensive, and I told her so. 'They are fit for a queen'. . . . Next day I bought them for her. You just can't imagine what it was like because all this took place long, long before you were born, in 1908, in Venice, when your aunt was so young, so . . ."

"Uncle, you're getting tired, you should rest."

"You're right, I'm tired. Leave me a while and take the small chest to your room. It's yours."

"But, uncle . . ."

"It's all yours, that's all! I trust I can give away whatever I want!"

His voice broke into a sob: the illusion was vanishing and he found himself again on the point of dying, of saying goodbye to the things he had loved. He turned to the wall and I left with the box in my hands, not knowing what to do.

On other occasions he would tell me about "the year of the famine," or "the year of the yellow corn," or "the year of the plague," and very old tales of murderers and ghosts. Once he even tried to sing a *corrido* from his youth, but it shattered in his jagged voice. He was leaving me his life, and he was happy. The doctor said that yes, he could see some recovery, but that we were not to raise our hopes, there was no cure, it was merely a matter of a few days more or less.

One afternoon of menacing dark clouds, when I was bringing in the clothes hanging out to dry in the courtyard, I heard Maria cry out. I stood still, listening to her cry as if it were a peal of thunder, the first of the storm to come. Then silence, and I was left alone in the courtyard, motionless. A bee buzzed by and the rain did not fall. No one knows as well as I do how awful a foreboding can be, a premonition hanging above a head turned towards the sky.

"Lichita, he's dying! He's gasping for air!"

"Go get the doctor. . . . No! I'll go. . . . But call Dona Clara to stay with you till I'm back."

"And the priest . . . fetch the priest."

I ran, I ran away from that unbearable moment, blunt and asphyxiating. I ran, hurried back, entered the house, made coffee; I greeted the relatives who began to arrive dressed in half-mourning; I ordered candles; I asked for a few holy relics; I kept on feverishly trying to fulfill my only obligation at the time, to be with my uncle. I asked the doctor: he had given him an injection, so as not to leave anything untried, but he knew it was useless. I saw the priest arrive with the Eucharist, even then I lacked the courage to enter. I knew I would regret it afterwards. *Thank God, now I won't die alone*—but I couldn't. I covered my face with my hands and prayed.

The priest came and touched my shoulder. I thought that all was over and I shivered.

"He's calling you. Come in."

I don't know how I reached the door. Night had fallen and the room, lit by a bedside lamp, seemed enormous. The furniture, larger than life, looked black, and a strange clogging atmosphere hung about the bed. Trembling, I felt I was inhaling death.

"Stand next to him," said the priest.

I obeyed, moving towards the foot of the bed, unable to look even at the sheets.

"Your uncle's wish, unless you say otherwise, is to marry you *in articulo mortis*, so that you may inherit his possessions. Do you accept?"

I stifled a cry of horror. I opened my eyes wide enough to

let in the whole terrible room. "Why does he want to drag me into his grave?" I felt death touching my skin.

"Luisa. . . ."

It was uncle Apolonio. Now I had to look at him. He could barely mouth the words, his jaw seemed slack and he spoke moving his face like that of a ventriloquist's doll.

". . . please."

And he fell silent with exhaustion.

I could take no more. I left the room. That was not my uncle, it did not even look like him. Leave everything to me, yes, but not only his possessions, his stories, his life . . . I didn't want it, his life, his death. I didn't want it. When I opened my eyes I was standing once again in the courtyard and the sky was still overcast. I breathed in deeply, painfully.

"Already? . . ." the relatives drew near to ask, seeing me so distraught.

I shook my head. Behind me, the priest explained.

"Don Apolonio wants to marry her with his last breath, so that she may inherit him."

"And you won't?" the old servant asked anxiously. "Don't be silly, you are the only one to deserve it. You were a daughter to them, and you have worked very hard looking after him. If you don't marry him, the cousins in Mexico City will leave you without a cent. Don't be silly!"

"It's a fine gesture on his part. . . ."

"And afterwards you'll be left a rich widow, as untouched as you are now." A young cousin laughed nervously.

"It's a considerable fortune, and I, as your uncle several times removed, would advise you to . . ."

"If you think about it, not accepting shows a lack of both charity and humility."

"That's true, that's absolutely true."

I did not want to give an old man his last pleasure, a pleasure I should, after all, be thankful for, because my youthful body, of which I felt so proud, had not dwelt in any of the regions of death. I was overcome by nausea. That was my last clear thought that night. I woke from a kind of hypnotic slumber as they forced me to hold his hand covered in cold sweat. I felt nauseous again, but said "yes."

I remember vaguely that they hovered over me all the time, talking all at once, taking me over there, bringing me over here, making me sign, making me answer. The taste of that night—a taste that has stayed with me for the rest of my life —was that of an evil ring-around-the-rosies turning vertiginously around me, while everyone laughed and sang grotesquely

> *This is the way the widow is wed,*
> *The widow is wed, the widow is wed*

while I stood, a slave, in the middle. Something inside me hurt, and I could not lift my eyes.

When I came to my senses, all was over, and on my hand shone the braided ring which I had seen so many times on my aunt Panchita's finger: there had been no time for anything else.

The guests began to leave.

"If you need me, don't hesitate to call. In the meantime give him these drops every six hours."

"May God bless you and give you strength."

"Happy honeymoon," whispered the young cousin in my ear, with a nasty laugh.

I returned to the sickbed. "Nothing has changed, nothing has changed." My fear certainly had not changed. I convinced Maria to stay and help me look after uncle Apolonio. I only calmed down once I saw dawn was breaking. It had started to rain, but without thunder or lightning, very still.

It kept on drizzling that day and the next, and the day after.

Four days of anguish. Nobody came to visit, nobody other than the doctor and the priest. On days like these no one goes out, everyone stays indoors and waits for life to start again. These are the days of the spirit, sacred days.

If at least the sick man had needed plenty of attention my hours would have seemed shorter, but there was little that could be done for him.

On the fourth night Maria went to bed in a room close by, and I stayed alone with the dying man. I was listening to the monotonous rain and praying unconsciously, half asleep and unafraid, waiting. My fingers stopped working, turning the rosary, and as I held the beads I could feel through my fingertips a peculiar warmth, a warmth both alien and intimate, the warmth we leave in things and which is returned to us transformed, a comrade, a brother foreshadowing the warmth of others, a warmth both unknown and recollected, never quite grasped and yet inhabiting the core of my bones. Softly, deliciously, my nerves relaxed, my fingers felt light, I fell asleep.

I must have slept many hours: it was dawn when I woke up. I knew because the lights had been switched off and the electric plant stops working at two in the morning. The room, barely lit by an oil lamp at the feet of the Holy Virgin on the chest of drawers, made me think of the wedding night, my wedding night. . . . It was so long ago, an empty eternity.

From the depth of the gloomy darkness don Apolonio's broken and tired breathing reached me. There he still was, not the man himself, simply the persistent and incomprehensible shred that hangs on, with no goal, with no apparent motive. Death is frightening, but life mingled with death, soaked in death, is horrible in a way that owes little to either life or death. Silence, corruption of the flesh, the stench, the monstrous transformation, the final vanishing act, all this is painful, but it reaches a climax and then gives way, dissolves into the earth, into memory, into history. But not this: this arrangement worked out between life and death—echoed in the useless exhaling and inhaling—could carry on forever. I would hear him trying to clear his anaesthetized throat and it occurred to me that air was not entering that body, or rather, that it was not a human body breathing the air: it was a machine, puffing and panting, stopping in a curious game, a game to kill time without end. That thing was no human being: it was somebody playing with huffs and snores. And the horror of it all won me over: I began to breathe to the rhythm of his panting; to inhale, stop suddenly, choke, breathe, choke again . . . unable to control myself, until I realized I had been deceived by what I thought was the sense of the game. What I really felt was the pain and shortness of breath of an animal in pain. But I kept on, on, until there was one single breathing, one single inhuman breath, one single agony. I felt calmer, terrified but calmer: I had lifted the barrier, I could let myself go and simply wait for the common end. It seemed to me that by abandoning myself, by giving myself up unconditionally, the end would happen quickly, would not be allowed to continue. It would have fulfilled its purpose and its persistent search in the world.

Not a hint of farewell, not a glimmer of pity towards me. I carried on the mortal game for a long, long while, from someplace where time had ceased to matter.

The shared breathing became less agitated, more peaceful, but also weaker. I seemed to be drifting back. I felt so tired I could barely move, exhaustion nestling in forever inside my body. I opened my eyes. Nothing had changed.

No: far away, in the shadows, is a rose. Alone, unique, alive. There it is, cut out against the darkness, clear as day, with its fleshy, luminous petals, shining. I look at it and my hand moves and I remember its touch and the simple act of putting it in a vase. I looked at it then, but I only understand it now. I stir, I blink, and the rose is still there, in full bloom, identical to itself.

I breathe freely, with my own breath. I pray, I remember,

I doze off, and the untouched rose mounts guard over the dawning light and my secret. Death and hope suffer change.

And now day begins to break and in the clean sky I see that at last the days of rain are over. I stay at the window a long time, watching everything change in the sun. A strong ray enters me and the suffering seems a lie. Unjustified bliss fills my lungs and unwittingly I smile. I turn to the rose as if to an accomplice but I can't find it: the sun has withered it.

Clear days came again, and maddening heat. The people went to work, and sang, but don Apolonio would not die; in fact he seemed to get better. I kept on looking after him, but no longer in a cheerful mood—my eyes downcast, I turned the guilt I felt into hard work. My wish, now clearly, was that it all end, that he die. The fear, the horror I felt looking at him, at his touch, his voice, were unjustified because the link between us was not real, could never be real, and yet he felt like a dead weight upon me. Through politeness and shame I wanted to get rid of it.

Yes, don Apolonio was visibly improving. Even the doctor was surprised and offered no explanation.

On the very first morning I sat him up among the pillows, I noticed that certain look in my uncle's eyes. The heat was stifling and I had to lift him all by myself. Once I had propped him up I noticed: the old man was staring as dazed at my heaving chest, his face distorted and his trembling hands unconsciously moving towards me. I drew back instinctively and turned my head away.

"Please close the blinds, it's too hot."

His almost dead body was growing warm.

"Come here, Luisa, sit by my side. Come."

"Yes, uncle." I sat, my knees drawn up, at the foot of the bed, without looking at him.

"Polo, you must call me Polo." His voice was again sweet

and soft. "You'll have a lot to forgive me. I'm old and sick, and a man in my condition is like a child."

"Yes."

"Let's see. Try saying, 'Yes, Polo.' "

"Yes, Polo."

The name on my lips seemed to me an aberration, made me nauseated.

Polo got better, but became fussy and irritable. I realized he was fighting to be the man he had once been, and yet the resurrected self was not the same, but another.

"Luisa, bring me . . . Luisa, give me . . . Luisa, plump up my pillows . . . pour me some water . . . prop up my leg. . . ."

He wanted me to be there all day long, always by his side, seeing to his needs, touching him. And the fixed look and distorted face kept coming back, more and more frequently, growing over his features like a mask.

"Pick up my book. It fell underneath the bed, on this side."

I kneeled and stuck my head and almost half my body underneath the bed, and had to stretch my arm as far as it would go, to reach it. At first I thought it had been my own movements, or maybe the bedclothes, but once I had the book in my hand and was shuffling to get out, I froze, stunned by what I had long foreseen, even expected: the outburst, the scream, the thunder. A rage never before felt raced through me when the realization of what was happening reached my consciousness, when his shaking hand, taking advantage of my amazement, became surer and heavier, and enjoyed itself, adventuring with no restraints, feeling and exploring my thighs—a fleshless hand glued to my skin, fingering my body with delight, a dead hand searching impatiently between my legs, a bodyless hand.

I rose as quickly as I could, my face burning with shame and determination, but when I saw him I forgot myself: he had become a figure in a nightmare. Polo was laughing softly, through his toothless mouth. And then, suddenly serious, with a coolness that terrified me, he said:

"What? Aren't you my wife before God and men? Come here, I'm cold, heat my bed. But first take off your dress, you don't want to get it creased."

What followed, I know, is my story, my life, but I can barely remember it; like a disgusting dream I can't even tell whether it was long or short. Only one thought kept me sane during the early days: "This can't go on, it can't go on." I imagined that God would not allow it, would prevent it in some way or another. He, personally, God, would interfere. Death, once dreaded, seemed my only hope. Not Apolonio's—he was a demon of death—but mine, the just and necessary death for my corrupted flesh. But nothing happened. Everything stayed on, suspended in time, without future. Then, one morning, taking nothing with me, I left.

It was useless. Three days later they let me know that my husband was dying, and they called me back. I went to see the father confessor and told him my story.

"What keeps him alive is lust, the most horrible of all sins. This isn't life, Father, it's death. Let him die!"

"He would die in despair. I can't allow it."

"And I?"

"I understand, but if you don't go to him, it would be like murder. Try not to arouse him, pray to the Blessed Virgin, and keep your mind on your duties. . . ."

I went back. And lust drew him out of the grave once more. Fighting, endlessly fighting, I managed, after several years, to overcome my hatred, and finally, at the very end, I even conquered the beast: Apolonio died in peace, sweetly, his old self again.

But I was not able to go back to who I was. Now wickedness, malice, shine in the eyes of the men who look at me, and I feel I have become an occasion of sin for all, I, the vilest of harlots. Alone, a sinner, totally engulfed by the never-ending flames of this cruel summer which surrounds us all, like an army of ants.

Translated by Alberto Manguel

The Guerrillero

ALBALUCÍA ANGEL

IT WAS THE POET Ana Becciú who introduced me to the works
of the Colombian writer Albalucía Angel. The literature of
Colombia has suffered from the overwhelming shadow of Gabriel García Márquez, whose name has become synonymous
not only with all of that country's writing but also with that
of the rest of Latin America. Albalucía Angel's work shares no
common ground with that of García Márquez. Her stories are
not sweeping pageants; they are snapshots of a character's
life, moments captured out of context, scenes rather than
complete biographies. Her novel Dos veces Alicia (Twice
Alice) echoes the voice of Lewis Carroll, both in its dreamlike
plot and in the invention of a language, making readers believe that what they are following is a demented detective
story. "The Guerrillero" is a more traditional tale, which
nevertheless preserves the looking-glass quality of the novel:
it is told by a woman speaking to herself, author becoming
character, reflecting as she does the sordid background of
her country's political landscape.

Now you'll see, Felicidad Mosquera, when they all arrive
with their machetes, threatening, asking you where in hell
has he hidden himself, then you'll confess. They'll ask.
They'll force you to betray him because if you won't talk
they'll take the old folks, like they did two days ago with your
friend Cleta, remember, or they'll put your hands into the
fire, like Calixta Peñalosa, or they'll slice open your belly,
after all—all of them—have used your body. That's how it is,
Felicidad. That's how it is. You should have gone with him,
then you wouldn't have suffered. You wouldn't be dragging
yourself around, crying and moaning, looking for anything
that might do as a weapon, pushing the few bits of furniture
against the door. That night, when Sebastian Martinez's dogs
began to howl as if they'd smelled the devil, and you saw him
there, suddenly, standing ever so still, his trousers in shreds
and his white shirt all bloody, then you should have spoken,
said anything, any excuse to make him whisper good-night
and creep back where he'd come from, but no, too bad it
didn't happen that way. Bad luck, Felicidad. You made him
come in without a word, you pulled up a chair for him, he let
himself fall heavy as lead, and then you saw the other wound
on his skull; *I'm tired*, was all he mumbled; and then col-
lapsed like a horse on the floor. Whatever got into your head,
Felicidad Mosquera? What evil star dazzled you then, what
evil wind blew through your heart to stir up the fire, to blind
you? Because you were blind, blind. The shivers you felt
when you looked upon his face and realized he was so hand-
some. That you liked his black moustache. The nervous urgency with which you went to boil water and prepare the herb
plasters, somehow wasn't yours. Because you've always been
cool-headed. A watchful heart. Careful. You never let yourself be trapped into these things. Whatever happened to you,
tell me. Whatever came over you when instead of saying
good-bye, once he felt better, and began to go out at night to

take a walk, to get firewood, offering to pump water, instead of saying yes, well thank you, see you sometime, you said no, it was no trouble, why didn't he stay a few more days. What happened, damn you. I can't understand. Felicidad Mosquera, I don't recognize you any longer. I never thought you'd change this fast, go from black to white, as you did, from one day to the other. Because the trembling you felt when he looked at you with his dark eyes, or the stammering, like a little girl, when he asked for the salt and barely touched you with his fingers as you put it in his hand, everything in you turned upside-down, the current changed, your cables crossed, so how in God's name didn't you notice it. Putting salt into another person's hand is stupid, brings bad luck. Bad tidings. And what about that day when instead of letting him go off on his own to get some air, you flushed, all red in the face, when he offered to walk together for a while, and crossing the bridge he held your waist, because it shakes so much was his excuse, but you felt how the heat boiling on his skin began to seep into you, burning, hurting, a cry inside you. A deep, deep moan. They're coming, Felicidad Mosquera. They'll come shouting that they know. Kicking everything in the house, as they did with Prospero Montoya's wife, when they left her stuck inside the well, her belly sliced open and the baby inside. They won't let you make the slightest move. When they arrive like that they're all ready to kill you. To leave no trace. They'll say they know so that you go for it. But only God and you are witnesses. The only witnesses of the meeting in the fields, on the river bank, between the scented sheets; who else will swear if only you felt the delight, the sex entering your body, searching your smoothness, changing you into streams, twilight, sea; who else will know the movement of your thighs, burning, your hands searching; touching the groin forcing sweetly your way into life. Who else heard his groans. His loving search. His long, drawn-out orgasm as you sank into a silence of moist membranes, a quick throb of blood, a hurried quiver of muscles, which then relaxed rippling through the entire body, an inside scream bursting upwards, like a torrent. And who's to judge you, Felicidad Mosquera, if only God and you can swear that this is true. No one will dare. They can search your very innards, cut you in two with their machetes, drill into your senses, pierce your heart, they will find nothing. Not a whisper. Don't look like that. Throw your fear overboard. Don't curse any more: he's far away and all that counts is that he lives and carries on fighting. You won't say a word. Not even if they set fire to your shack, ram themselves into you, or bottles, or do what they did to others to drive you crazy; take courage, Felicidad Mosquera, don't cry or moan any more. Open the door yourself. Stand upright in the doorway. Hold their eyes.

Translated by Alberto Manguel

Haute Cuisine

AMPARO DÁVILA

DURING THE SPANISH reign in Latin America, fiction was not allowed into the New World. Only descriptions of "reality"— reality seen through the eyes of Europeans fed on the medieval imagination—were permitted to circulate freely. The New World as seen by the Europeans was populated by the creatures their imagination demanded. Pliny had described mermaids; Montaigne had explained the manners of imaginary cannibals; every bestiary had its unicorns and dragons, and all these beings found a home in the land Columbus believed to be the Indies. This is also the world of Amparo Dávila, a world "contaminated by nightmares," as she once described it. Her childhood was spent among nuns and miners; she began to write poetry in school before the age of ten. Her stories, written after she moved to Mexico City in the 1950s, describe the struggles of family life, the strictures of society that affect not only men and women but also—as in "Haute Cuisine"—their dreams and the creatures in their dreams.

WHEN I HEAR the rain lashing against my window, their cries come back to me once again, those cries that used to stick to my skin like leeches. Their pitch would increase as the pot heated up and the water began to boil. And I also see their eyes, small, beady and black, popping from their sockets when they were cooked.

They were born during the rainy season, in the vegetable gardens. Hidden among the leaves, gripping onto the stalks, or lurking in the wet grass. From there they were torn off to be sold, and at a good price, too. Three for five cents usually, and when there were many, at fifteen cents a dozen.

At home we used to buy about two pesos' worth every week, being as it was the established Sunday dish, and even more often than that if we had guests. My family would only serve it to distinguished or well-loved visitors. "Nowhere else do they prepare them as well," my mother used to say, so proudly, when complimented on her cooking.

I remember the gloomy kitchen and the pot in which they were cooked—a pot fashioned and burnished by an old French chef—the wooden spoon dusky with age, and the cook, a fat, ruthless woman, unmoved by their suffering. The heart-rending cries did not affect her; she would carry on fanning the fire, blowing on the coals as if nothing were happening. From my room in the attic I could hear them shriek. It was always raining, and their cries would mix with the patter of the rain. They took ages to die. To me, it seemed as if their agony would go on forever. I would stay in my room, my head buried beneath my pillow, but even beneath the pillow I could hear them. Sometimes I would wake up at midnight and go on hearing them. I never knew whether they were still alive, or whether their cries had stayed on inside me, inside my head, inside my ears, inside and outside, hammering away, tearing me apart.

Sometimes I would see hundreds of little eyes glued to the

dripping window-panes. Hundreds of black, round eyes. Shining eyes, wet with tears, begging for mercy. But there was no mercy in our house. No one felt moved by our cruelty. Their eyes and their cries would follow me—as they follow me even today—everywhere I went.

A few times they sent me out to buy them. I would always return empty-handed, swearing that I had not found any. One day they began to suspect, and I was never sent again. The cook would go instead. She would return with a pailful, and I would look at her full of contempt as one would look at the cruelest executioner. She would wrinkle her pug nose and snort superciliously.

Preparing them was a complicated task and took time. First she would put them in a box lined with grass, and give them a certain rare herb that they would eat—seemingly with pleasure—and that acted as a purgative. There they would spend the first day. On the following morning she would bathe them carefully so as not to harm them, she would dry them, and she would place them in the pot full of cold water, spices, aromatic herbs, salt and vinegar.

When the water began to heat they would start shrieking, shrieking, shrieking. . . . They would shriek like newborn babies, like squashed mice, like bats, like strangled kittens, like hysterical women.

On that occasion—my last day at home—the banquet was long and exquisite.

Translated by Alberto Manguel

The Night Visitor

ELENA PONIATOWSKA

REALISTIC FICTION IN Mexico today is a direct issue of the Mexican Revolution, which began in 1810 with the rebellion of a parish priest and ended in 1917 with the republican constitution that put an end to the civil war. The upper class, against whom the revolution had been directed, continued however to hold its autocratic rule, and the fate of Indians and peasants did not improve. Agustin Yañez, Juan Rulfo, and Carlos Fuentes became the first chroniclers of their history. Elena Poniatowska belongs to this realistic tradition. The daughter of a Polish nobleman, Elena Poniatowska was born in France and came to Mexico at the age of ten. She began her writing career as a journalist; her first-hand experience of Mexico City's lower depths inspired her to write a novel, Hasta no verte, Jesús mío *(See You Never, Sweet Jesus), the fictionalized biography of a laundress, an urban child of the revolution. Poniatowska's style is direct, built of precise images and authentic-sounding dialogue, and is less baroque than Fuentes's style, more complex than Yañez's. The following story is from a collection soon to be published in English.*

"BUT, YOU . . . don't you suffer?"

"Me?"

"Yes, you."

"A little, sometimes, like when my shoes are tight. . . ."

"I'm referring to your situation, Mrs. Loyden." He stressed the Mrs., letting it fall to the bottom of Hell, Miss-sus, and all it implied. "Don't you suffer because of it?"

"No."

"Wasn't it a lot of trouble to get where you are? Your family went to a good deal of expense?"

The woman shifted in her seat. Her green eyes no longer questioned the Public Ministry agent. She looked at the tips of her shoes. These didn't hurt her. She used them every day.

"Don't you work in an institution that grew out of the Mexican Revolution? Haven't you benefitted from it? Don't you enjoy the privileges of a class that yesterday had scarcely arrived from the fields and today receives schooling, medical attention, and social welfare? You've been able to rise, thanks to your work. Oh, I forgot. You have a curious concept of work."

The woman protested in a clear voice, even though its intonations were childish.

"I'm a registered nurse. I can show you my license. Right now, if we go to my house."

"Your house?" said the Public Ministry agent ironically, "Your house? Which of your houses?"

The judge was old, pure worm-eaten wood, painted and repainted, but, strangely, the face of this Public Ministry agent didn't look so old, in spite of his curved shoulders and the shudders that shook them. His voice was old, his intentions old. His gestures were clumsy as was his way of fixing his eyes on her through his glasses and getting irritated like a teacher with a student who hasn't learned his lesson. "Objects contaminate people," she thought. "This man looks like a piece of paper, a drawer, an inkwell. Poor fellow." Behind her in the other armchairs there was no one, just a policeman scratching his crotch near the exit door, which opened to admit a short woman who reached up to the Public Ministry agent's desk and handed him a document. After looking at it, he admonished her in a loud voice, "The crimes must be classified correctly. . . . And at the end, you always forget the 'Effective Suffrage, No Re-Election.' Don't let it happen again, please!"

When they were alone, the accused inquired in her high voice, "Could I call home?"

The judge was about to repeat sharply, "Which one?" But he preferred a negative. He rounded his mouth in such a way that the wrinkles converged like they do on a chicken's ass.

"No."

"Why?"

"Because we-are-in-the-mid-dle-of-an-in-ter-ro-ga-tion. We are making a deposition."

"Oh, and if I have to go to the bathroom, do I have to wait?"

"My God, is this woman mentally retarded, or what? But if she were, how could she have received her diploma?"

He inquired with renewed curiosity, "To whom do you wish to speak?"

"My father."

"Her father . . . her-fa-ther," he mocked. "To top it off, you have a father!"

"Yes," she said, swinging her legs, "Yes, my daddy is still alive."

"Really? And does your father know what kind of a daughter he has?"

"I'm very much like him," said the child-woman with a smile. "We've always looked alike. Always."

"Really? And when do you see him, if you please?"

"Saturdays and Sundays. I try to spend the weekends with him."

The sweetness of her tone made the policeman stop scratching himself.

"Every Saturday and Sunday?"

"Well, not always. Sometimes an emergency comes up, and I don't go. But I always let him know by phone."

"And the others? Do you let them know?"

"Yes."

"Don't waver, madam. You're in a court of law."

The woman looked with candid eyes at the ten empty chairs behind her, the wooden counter painted gray, and the high file cabinets, government issue. On passing through the rooms on the way to the Public Ministry agent's office, the metal desks almost overwhelmed her. They too were covered with files piled every which way, some with a white card between the pages as a marker. She almost knocked down one of the tall stacks perched dangerously on a corner in front of a fat woman eating her lunch, elbows on her desk. It was obvious that she had previously bitten into a sandwich, and now she was gleefully adding greasy pieces of avocado to the opened bread cut with the paper knife. The floor of the grayish, worn out granite was filthy even though it was mopped daily. Windows that looked out on the street were very small and had thick, closely spaced bars. The dirty panes let through a sad, grime-choked light. It was clear that no one cared about the building, that everyone fled from it as soon as work was finished. No air entered the offices except through the door to the street that closed immediately. The fat lady put the remains of her sandwich that she meant to finish later in a brown paper bag where there also was a banana. The drawer shut with a coiled-spring sound. Then, with greasy hands, she faced her typewriter. All the machines were tall, very old, and the ribbons never returned by themselves. The fat lady put her finger into the carriage—the nail of her little finger—and began to return it. Then she got tired. With an inky finger, she pulled open the middle desk drawer and took out a ballpoint pen that she put in the center of the ribbon. When she finished—now with her glasses on—she started work without bothering about the defendant in the antechamber reading the accusation: "The witness affirms that he wasn't at home at the time of the events. . . ." The typist stopped to adjust the copies, wetting her thumb and index finger. All the documents were made with ten copies when five would do. That's why there was a great deal of used carbons with government initials in the square gray wastebaskets. "Oh, boy, what a lot of carbon paper! What do they want with so many copies?" Everyone in the tribunal seemed immune to criticism. Some scratched their sides, others their armpits, women fixed a bra strap, grimacing. They grimaced on sitting down, but once seated they got up again to go to another desk to consult whatever it was that made them scratch their noses or pass their tongues several times over their teeth looking for some prodigious milligram. Once they found it, they took it out with their little finger. All in all, if they weren't aware of what they were doing, they weren't aware of the others either.

"Have them send Garcia to take a deposition."

"How many copies will they make?" asked the accused.

Nothing altered the clearness of her gaze, no shadow, no hidden motive on the shining surface.

The Public Ministry agent had to respond, "Ten."

"I knew it!"

"So, how many times have you been arrested?"

"None. This is the first time. I knew it because I noticed when we came in. I'm very observant," she said with a satisfied smile.

"You must be in order to have done what you've done for seven years."

She smiled, a fresh innocent smile, and the judge thought,

"It's easy to see. . . ." He almost smiled. "I must keep this impersonal. But how can it be done when this woman seems to be playing, crossing and uncrossing her legs, showing her golden, round, perfectly shaped knees?"

"Let's see . . . your name is . . ."

"Esmeralda Loyden."

"Age?"

"Twenty-seven."

"Place of birth?"

"Mexico City."

"Native?"

"Yes." Esmeralda smiled again.

"Address?"

"27 Mirto, Apartment 3."

"District?"

"Santa Maria la Rivera."

"Postal zone?"

"Four."

"Occupation?"

"Nurse. Listen, Your Honor, the address I gave you is my father's." She shook her curly head. "You have the other ones."

"All right. Now we're going to look at your declaration. Are you getting this down, Garcia?"

"Yes, Your Honor."

"Catholic?"

"Yes."

"Practicing?"

"Yes."

"When?"

"I always go to mass on Sunday, Your Honor."

"Oh, really? And how is your conscience?"

"Fine, your honor. I especially like singing masses."

"And midnight masses? You must like those best," the old man said hoarsely.

"That's only once a year, but I like them, too."

"Oh, really? And who do you go with?"

"My father. I try to spend Christmas with him."

Esmeralda's green eyes, like tender, untrodden grass, got bigger.

"She almost looks like a virgin," thought the agent.

"Let's see, Garcia. We're ready to pronounce sentence in Case 132/6763, Thirtieth Tribunal, Second Penal Court on five counts of bigamy."

"Five, your honor?"

"It's five, isn't it?"

"Yes, your honor, but only one accuses her."

"But she's married to five of them, isn't she?"

"Yes, sir."

"Put it down. Then, let's look at the first statement from Queretaro, State of Queretaro. It says, "United States of Mexico. In the name of the Mexican Republic and as Civil State Judge of this place I make known to those witnesses now present and certify to be true that in the Book titled Marriages of the Civil Registry in my jurisdiction, on page 18, of the year 1948, permission of government number 8577, File 351.2/49/82756 of the date June 12, 1948, F.M. at 8:00 P.M., before me appeared the citizens, Pedro Lugo and Miss Esmeralda Loyden with the object of matrimony under the rule of conjugal society.' Are you getting this, Garcia? Like this one, there are four more certificates, all properly certified and sealed. Only the names of the male correspondents change because the female correspondent—horrors—is always the same: Esmeralda Loyden. Here is a document signed in Cuernavaca, Morelos; another in Chilpancingo, Guerrero; another in Los Mochis, Sinaloa; and the fifth in Guadalajara, Jalisco. It appears that, as well as bigamy, you like traveling, madam."

"Not so much, Your Honor. They're the ones that . . . well, you know, for the honeymoon."

"Ah, yes."

"Yes, Your Honor. If it had been up to me, I would have stayed in Mexico City." Her voice was melodious.

The short woman entered again with the folder. The exasperated agent opened it and read aloud, " '. . . with visual inspections and ministerial faith, so much of the injury caused during the course of the above mentioned events in the clause immediately before . . .' Now you can go on from there yourself. It's only a copy . . . Ah, and look! You forgot the 'Effective Suffrage, No Re-election' again. Didn't I tell you? Well, watch what you're doing. Don't let it happen again . . . please."

When the dwarf shut the door, the judge hurried to say, "The names of the male parties, Garcia, must appear in the Juridical Edict in strict alphabetical order. Carlos Gonzales, Pedro Lugo, Gabriel Mercado, Livio Martinez, Julio Vallarta . . . one . . . two . . . three . . . four . . . five." The judge counted to himself. . . . "So you're Mrs. Esmeralda Loyden Gonzalez, Mrs. Esmeralda Loyden Lugo, Mrs. Esmeralda Loyden Martinez, Mrs. Esmeralda Loyden Mercado, Mrs. Esmeralda Loyden Vallarta. . . . Hmmm. How does that sound to you, Garcia?"

"Fine."

"What do you mean, fine?"

"The names are all correct, Your Honor, but the only one who's accusing her is Pedro Lugo."

"I'm not asking you that, Garcia. I am pointing out the moral, legal, social and political implications of the case. They seem to escape you."

"Oh, that, Your Honor!"

"Have you ever encountered, Garcia, in your experience, a case like this?"

"No, Your Honor. Well, not with a woman because with men . . ." Garcia whistled in the air, a long whistle, like a passing train.

"Let's see what the accused has to say. But before that, let me ask you a personal question, Mrs. Esmeralda. Didn't you get Julio confused with Livio?"

Esmeralda appeared like a child in front of a marvelous kaleidoscope. She looked through the transparent waters of her eyes. It was a kaleidoscope only she could see. The judge, indignant, repeated his question, and Esmeralda jumped as if the question startled her.

"Get them confused? No, Your Honor. They're all very different!"

"You never had a doubt, a slip up?"

"How could I?" she responded energetically. "I respect them too much."

"Not even in the dark?"

"I don't understand."

She rested a clear, tranquil gaze on the old man, and the agent was taken aback.

"It's incredible," he thought. "Incredible. Now I'm the one who'll have to beg her pardon!"

Then he attacked. "Did she undergo a gynecological exam with the court doctor?"

"Why, no," protested Garcia. "It's not a question of rape."

"Ah, yes, that's true. They're the ones who have to have it," laughed the agent, rubbing his hands together.

The woman also laughed as if it had nothing to do with her. She laughed to be kind, to keep the old man company. This disconcerted him even more.

"So there are five?" He tapped on the grimy wooden table.

"Five of them needed me."

"And you were able to accommodate them?"

"They had a considerable urgency."

"And children? Do you have children?" he asked almost respectfully.

"How could I? They are my children. I take care of them

and help them with everything. I wouldn't have time for others."

The judge couldn't go on. Jokes with double meaning, vulgarities, witty comments all went over her head. . . . And Garcia was a hairy beast, an ox. He even appeared to have gone over to her side. That was the limit! He couldn't be thinking of becoming. . . . The agent would have to wait until he was at the saloon with his cronies to tell them about this woman who smiled simply because smiling was part of her nature.

"I suppose you met the first one in the park."

"How did you know? Yes, I met Carlos in the Sunken Park. I was there reading Jose Emilio Pacheco's novel, *You Will Die Far Away*."

"So, you like to read?"

"No. He's the only one I've read and that's because I've met him." Esmeralda perked up. "I thought he was a priest. Imagine. We shared the same taxi, and when he got out I said, 'Father, give me your blessing.' He got very nervous and was even sweating. He handed me something black, 'Look. So you'll see I'm not what you think, I'm giving you my book.' "

"Well, what happened with Carlos?"

"Pedro . . . I mean, Carlos sat down on the bench where I was reading and asked me if the book was good. That's how everything started. Oh, no! Then something got in his eye— you know February is the month for dust storms. I offered to get it out for him. His eye was full of tears. I told him I was a nurse and then . . . I got it out. Listen, by the way, I've noticed that your left eye has been watering. Why don't you tell your wife to put some chamomile in it, not the kind from a package, but the fresh kind, with a good flower. Tell your wife . . . if I could I would do it for you. You have to make sure the cup is quite clean before boiling a tiny bit of chamomile of the good kind. Then you hold yourself like this with your head thrown back. About ten minutes, so it penetrates well. . . . You'll see how it soothes. Pure chamomile flower."

"So, you're the kind who offers herself . . . to help."

"Yes, Your Honor. It's my natural reaction. The same thing happened with Gabriel. He'd burned his arm. You should have seen how awful, one pustule after another. I treated it. It was my job to bandage him as ordered by Dr. Carrillo. Then when he was well, he told me—I don't know how many times—that what he loved best in the world—besides me—was his right arm because it was the reason. . . ."

Esmeralda Loyden's five tales were similar. One case followed another with little variation. She related her marriages with shining, confident eyes. Sometimes, she was innocently conceited. "Pedro can't live without me. He doesn't even know where his shirts are." On the Public Ministry agent's lips trembled the words "perversion," "perfidy," "depravity," "absolute shame." But an opportunity never arose to voice them even though they were burning his tongue. With Esmeralda they lost all meaning. Her story was simple, without artifice. Mondays were Pedro's. Tuesdays Carlos's, and so on . . . until the week was complete. Saturdays and Sundays were set aside for washing and ironing clothes and preparing some special dish for Pedro, the most capricious of the five. When an emergency came up, a birthday, a saint's day, an outing, she gave up a Saturday or Sunday. No, no. They accepted everything, as long as they saw her. The only condition she always put was not giving up her nursing career.

"And they were agreeable to only having one day?"

"Sometimes they get an extra day. Besides, they work, too. Carlos is a traveling salesman, but manages to be in the City on Wednesdays. He doesn't miss those. Gabriel sells insurance. He also travels and is so intelligent they've offered him a job with IBM."

"None of them has ever wanted a child?"

"They never said so in so many words. When they talk about it, I tell them we've only been together a few years, that love matures."

"They accept this?"

"Yes, apparently."

"Well, apparently not. Now your game's up because they've denounced you."

"That was Pedro, the most temperamental, the most excitable. But at heart, Your Honor, he's a good fellow. He's generous. You know, like milk that boils over, then settles down. . . . You'll see."

"I'm not going to see anything because you are confined to jail. You've been separated for eight days. Or haven't you noticed, Mrs. Loyden? Don't you regret being locked up?"

"Not much. Everyone's very nice. Besides you lose track of time. I've slept at least eight hours a night. I was really tired."

"I imagine so. . . . Then things haven't gone badly for you?"

"No. I've never lost sleep from worrying."

And really, the girl looked good, her skin healthy and clean, her eyes shining with health, all of her a calm smoothness. Ah! Her hair also shone, hair like that of a newborn animal, fine hair that invited caressing, just as her turned up nose invited tweaking. The judge started furiously. He was fed up with so much nonsense.

"Don't you realize you lived in absolute promiscuity? You deceived. You de-ceive. Not only are you immoral, but amoral. You don't have principles. You're pornographic. Yours is a case of mental illness. Your naïveté is a sign of imbecility. Your . . . your . . ."—he began to stutter—"People like you undermine the base of our society. You destroy the family nucleus. You're a social menace! Don't you realize all the wrong you've done with your irresponsible conduct?"

"Wrong to who?" cried Esmeralda.

"The men you've deceived, yourself, society, the principles of the Mexican Revolution!"

"Why? Shared days are happy days! Harmonious. They don't hurt anyone!"

"And the deceit?"

"What deceit? It's one thing not to say anything. It's another to deceive."

"You're crazy. Moreover, the psychiatrist is going to prove it. For sure."

"Really? Then what will happen to me?"

"Ah, hah! Now you're worried! It's the first time you've thought about your fate."

"Yes, Your Honor. I've never been a worrier."

"What kind of a woman are you? I don't understand you. Either you're mentally deficient . . . or . . . I don't know . . . a loose woman."

"Loose woman?"—Esmeralda got serious—"Tell Pedro that."

"Pedro, Juan, and the others. When they find out, they're going to think the same thing."

"They won't think the same thing. They're all different. I don't think the same as you, and I couldn't if I wanted to."

"Don't you realize your lack of remorse?"

The agent hit his fist on the table making the age-old dust fly. "You're a wh . . . You act like a pros . . . (Curiously, he couldn't say the words in front of her. Her smile inhibited him. Looking at her closely . . . he'd never seen such a pretty girl. She wasn't so pretty at first sight, but she grew in healthiness, cleanliness, freshness. She seemed to have just bathed. That was it. What would she smell like? Perhaps like vanilla? A woman with all her teeth. You could see them when she threw her head back to laugh, because the shameless woman laughed.)

"Well, and don't you sometimes see yourself as trash?"

"Me?" she asked, surprised. "Why?"

The agent felt disarmed.

"Garcia, call Lucita to take a statement."

Lucita was the one with the avocado and the banana. She carried her shorthand tablet under her arm, her finger still covered with ink. She sat down grimacing and muttered, "The defendant. . . ."

"No, look. Do it directly on the machine. It comes out better. What have you to say in your defense, Mrs. Loyden?"

"I don't know legal terms. I wouldn't know how to say it. Why don't you advise me, Your Honor, since you're so knowledgable?

"It . . . it . . . it's too much," stuttered the agent, "Now I have to advise her. Read the file, Lucita."

Lucita opened a folder with a white card in the middle and said, "It's not signed."

"If you like," proposed Esmeralda, "I'll sign it."

"You haven't made a statement yet. How are you going to sign it?"

"It doesn't matter. I'll sign beforehand. After all, Gabriel told me that in the courts they write in whatever they want."

"Well, Gabriel's a liar, and I'm going to have the pleasure of sending him a subpoena accusing him of defamation."

"Will I be able to see him?" Esmeralda asked excitedly.

"Gabriel? I doubt very much he'll want to see you."

"But the day he comes, will you send for me?"

(Crazy, ignorant, animal-like, all women are crazy. They are vicious, degenerate, demented, bestial. To think she would get involved with five at a time and awaken fresh as the morning. Because the many nights on duty have not affected this woman at all. She doesn't even hear anything I say, for all I try to make her understand.)

"By that time you'll be behind bars in the Santa Marta

Acatitla prison. For desecration of morality, for bigamy, for not being wise"—he thought of various other possible crimes —"for injuries to particular individuals, criminal association, incitement to rebellion, attacks on public property. Yes, yes. Didn't you meet Carlos in the park."

"But, will I be able to see Gabriel?"

"Is he the one you love most?" asked the Public Minister, suddenly intrigued.

"No. I love them all, equally."

"Even Pedro who denounced you?"

"Oh, my sweet Pedro," she said rocking him between her breasts . . . which looked very firm because they stayed erect while she made the rocking gesture.

"That's the last straw!"

Lucita, with a pencil behind her ear, stuck in her greasy hair, crackled something in her hands, a brown paper bag. Perhaps so the agent would notice her or so he would stop shouting. For the past few moments, Lucita had been staring at the accused. In fact, four or five employees weren't missing a word of the confrontation. Carmelita left her *Tears and Laughs*, and Tere put away her photo novel. Carvajal was standing next to Garcia, and Perez and Mantecon were listening intently. In the courtroom, men wore ties, but everyone looked dirty and sweaty. Clothes stuck to them like poultices, their suits shiny and full of lint, and that horrible brown color that dark people like to wear. It makes them look like rancid chocolate. Lucita, though, fitted her short stature with screaming colors. A green skirt with a yellow nylon blouse, or was it the opposite? Pure circus combinations, but her face was so rapt now that she looked attractive. Interest ennobled them. They had quit scuffing their feet, scratching their bodies, and leaning against the walls. No indolence remained. They had come alive. They remembered they were once men, once young, once totally unattached to the paperwork and marking of cards. Drops of crystalline water shone on their foreheads. Esmeralda bathed them.

"The press is waiting outside," Lucita advised the Public Ministry agent.

He stood up. He wasn't in the habit of making the press wait. It was the fifth power.

Meanwhile, Lucita approached Esmeralda and patted her thigh. "Don't worry, honey. I'm with you. I'm enjoying this because the bastard I married had another woman after a while. He even put her up in a house, and he's got me here working. How terrific that someone like you can get revenge. I'll help on that last interrogation. I swear I'll help. And not only me, but Carmelita, too. That's her desk over there. And Carvajal and Mantecon and Perez and Mr. Michael, who's a little old-fashioned, but nice. What can I say? You're better than divine Yesenia for us. Let's see. I'll start the statement, 'the defendant. . . .' (By now, Esmeralda, convicted or not, felt a drowsiness that made her curl up in the chair like a cat whom everyone likes, especially Lucita.)

Lucita's keys flew joyously through the legal terms—written, they're obscure; spoken in a loud voice, they're incomprehensible. Lucita insisted on saying them out loud to Esmeralda to give proof of her loyalty. After typing, "Coordinated Services of Prevention and Social Adaptation," and realizing she got no response, Lucita spoke in Esmeralda's ear. "You're sleepy, honey. We're about done. I'll only need to add something about damages, a notification, and reprehension of the accused. It doesn't all fit. Oh, well, that's in accord with the law. Let'er know her rights and the time allowed for appeal. 'Dispatch,' I think it has a 't.' Oh, well. Now the warrants and extra copies. The word 'court' should be capitalized, but I didn't do it the other five times. It's not important. Okay, sweetie, sign it here and . . . listen. D'ya want a cold drink to perk you up? Here are the identifying markers.

A formal decree presumes you're guilty and off to prison, but don't pay any attention. We won't let it happen. We need a medical certificate and a corresponding certificate of court appraisal . . . the law's conclusions. They'll all be favorable. You'll see, honey. I'll take care of it. For you, nothing can go wrong."

In her cell, after a good soup with chicken wing and thigh, Esmeralda slept surrounded by sympathetic jailers. The next day, groups came to demonstrate, including feminine sectors of several political parties. Rene Cardona Junior wanted to make a film on the spot. The press had reported events in scandalous form. "Five, Like The Fingers On Her Hand," read the headline across eight columns in the police section. *Ovaciones*, in big black headlines, wrote "Five Winners And The Jockey Is A Woman." Three exclamation marks. An editorial writer somberly began his column ". . . Once more our primitive nature is confronted and put to the test." He went into detail about low instincts. Another writer, obviously a technician with a state agency, spoke of the multistratification of women; they were treated like objects; domestic work didn't allow them access to the higher realms of culture. There were other dangerous distortions which the readers promised to read later. All in all, it was a tiring day. Among the many visitors appeared two nuns, very excited. That didn't count nuns not wearing habits, progressive ones, usually French. There were many. "Oh, boy," thought Lucita, "What a day for us women! Even though Esmeralda might turn out a scapegoat, she's our rallying flag. Her struggle is ours as well."

The Public Ministry agent took it upon himself, seeing heated spirits, to throw cold water on them.

"The courtroom will be closed to the public."

Lucita disappeared behind the old typewriter with the ribbon she had to rewind by hand.

"In Iztapalapa, Federal District at 10:30 o'clock on the 22nd day, within the period of time specified by Article 19 of the Constitution, proceedings were initiated to resolve the juridical situation of Mrs. Esmeralda Loyden Gonzalez Lugo Martinez Mercado Vallarta whom the Public Minister accuses of committing five counts of adultery, considered bigamy, as described by Article 37, Paragraph 1 of the Penal Code of Penal Processes with the writ of damages presented by the accuser who in his civilian state is called Pedro Lugo, who, having sworn and having been warned in terms of the law to conduct himself truthfully, subject to sanctions applied to those who submit false testimony, declared the above to be his name, to be thirty-two years of age, married, Catholic, educated, employed, originally from Coatzacoalcos, state of Veracruz, who in the essential part of his accusation said that on Monday, May 28, when his wife did not arrive as she usually did at 8:00 P.M. on the dot on Mondays at their conjugal dwelling, located at 246 Patriotismo, Apartment 16, Colonia San Pedro of the Pines, Postal Zone 13, he went to look for her at the hospital where she said she worked and not finding her, he asked if she would be there the following night and was informed by the receptionist to go see the administration since her name did not appear on the night duty list, that she thought she probably worked during the day, but since she came on with the second shift she was not sure and could not tell him, since she got there la–"——here Lucita just put "la" because "later" didn't fit on the line and she let it go—"and therefore (on the next line) she saw the necessity of sending the plaintiff to the administration to get more information and that in the already mentioned administration the accuser was informed that the one he called his wife never worked the night shift, so the man had to be restrained, putting his hands behind his back, something two attendants had to do after being called by the director, who feared the man wasn't sane. They then saw the accuser leave staggering, beside himself, supporting himself on the walls since he did sustain with the witness sexual relations being her legitimate husband as testified by certificate number 13797, page 18, being the said a pubescent, fecund woman, when he married her seven years ago. Afterward the accuser proceeded to subsequent inquiries adding what remains explained in file number 347597, without the knowledge of the defendant and managed to find out that the other four husbands were in the same situation and whom he proceeded to inform of the 'quintuplicity' of the accused. The presumed penal responsibility of the accused in the commission of the crimes committed with an original and five copies (the original for Pedro Lugo, being he, the first and principle accuser) as charged by the Social Representation, is found accredited to this moment, with the same elements of proof mentioned, in the consideration that precedes, with an emphasis on the direct imputation that the offended party makes and above all, the affidavit concerning the clothes and personal objects of the defendant at the five addresses mentioned as well as the numerous personal details, photographic proofs, inscriptions on photographs, letters and love missives lavishly written by the accused, brought together by the aggrieved and above all, the indisputableness and authenticity of the marriage certificates and the resulting acts derived from the aforesaid. And it can be said according to the five and to the accused herself, the marriages were dutifully and entirely consummated, to the full satisfaction of all, in the physical person of Esmeralda Loyden, so-called nurse by profession. That the defendant emitted declarations that are not supported by any proof that makes them credible, but on the contrary, proven worthless because of the elements which were alluded to [alluded with two "l" 's], that the defendant didn't manifest remorse at any moment, neither did she seem to realize that she was charged with five crimes, that she didn't voice any objection except that she was sleepy, that the defendant submits with notable docility to the administering of all tests, allowing all the procedures to be carried out that are necessary for the clarification of the facts, as well as those advanced by the parties, in accordance with the parts III, IV, and V of Article 20 of the Federal Constitution, be it notified and put into effect, the nature and cause of the accusation. On the same date, the Secretary of the Factions Clerk swears that the term for the parties to offer more proof in the present cause begins on this June 20 and concludes on next July 12. I swear this document to be true and valid."

When the Public Ministry Agent was about to put his signature at the bottom of the document, he yelled angrily, "Lucita, what's wrong with you? You forgot the 'Effective Suffrage, No Re-Election' again!"

Afterward, everything was rumor. Some say Esmeralda left with her jailkeepers for the jail wagon, followed by the faithful Lucita, who had prepared her a sandwich for the trip; by Garcia, the scribe, who kissed her hand; and by the affectionate gaze of the Public Ministry agent.

On saying good-bye, the agent again urged as he took her two hands between his own, moving each and everyone with his words: "Esmeralda, look what happens when you get involved in such things. Listen to me. You're young. Get away from all this, Esmeralda. Be respectable. From now on, be proper."

Many spectators made the convicted woman smile when they applauded her gracious manner. Others, on the other hand, saw, in the middle of the crowd behind the gray wooden bannister, painted and repainted with an always thinner coat, Pedro Lugo, the accuser, pierce Esmeralda with his intense gaze. On the other side, some saw myopic Julio give her a friendly sign with his hand. Getting into the police wagon, Esmeralda didn't see Carlos, but did notice Livio with his shaved head and eyes filled with tears. She yelled to him, "Why did you cut it? You know I don't like short hair."

The journalists took notes. None of the husbands was missing, not even the travelling salesman. Authoritative voices said the five husbands had tried to stop the trial because they all wanted Esmeralda back. But the sentence was already dictated, and they couldn't appeal to the Supreme Court of Justice. The case had received too much publicity. Each one agreed, in turn, to conjugal visits at Santa Maria Acatitla. Things were nearly the same, *"de facto et in situ."* Before, they had seen her only one night a week. Now they all got together occasionally for Sunday visits. Each one brought a treat. They took a variety of things to please not only Esmeralda, but also Lucita, Carmelita, Tere, Garcia, Carvaal, Perez, Mantecon, and the Public Ministry agent, who from time to time quietly presented himself—he'd grown fond of Esmeralda's responses.

But from these facts a new case couldn't be made. Accusors and accused, judge and litigants, had repented of their haste in bringing the first action, number 479/32/875746, page 68. Everything, though, remained in the so-called book of life which is full of trivia and which preceded the book now used to note the facts. It has an ugly name: computer certification. I swear this document to be true and valid.

Effective Suffrage, No Re-Election

Translated by Catherine S. White-House

Two Reports

SILVINA OCAMPO

POET, PAINTER, SHORT-STORY *writer, and translator (of Ronsard and Emily Dickinson) Silvina Ocampo masters a style that has been recognized by Roger Caillois and Italo Calvino among others as one of the finest, most original in the Spanish language. Her interests lie in the exploration of the world of animals and children: the cruelty of their games, the perversity of their beauty. The naive style of her stories is deceptive. Horror is described in a matter-of-fact manner, in a simple, nursery-rhyme language that leads the reader into what seems a safe place but turns out to be the mouth of Hell. For many years, Silvina Ocampo collaborated with her husband, the novelist Adolfo Bioy Casares, and with Jorge Luis Borges, compiling anthologies that have become classics, sometimes incorporating samples of her own work. The following reports appeared in two such anthologies:* The Book of Heaven and Hell *and* Brief and Extraordinary Tales.

Report on Heaven and Hell

LIKE THE WAREHOUSES of the more important auctioneers, Heaven and Hell hold in their galleries heaps of objects that would surprise no one, because they are all objects which can usually be found in the ordinary households of this world. But it is inaccurate to speak only of objects: in these galleries are also cities, villages, gardens, mountains, valleys, suns, moons, winds, seas, stars, reflections, temperatures, tastes, perfumes, sounds, because eternity has in store for us all kinds of sensations and pageants.

If the wind roars in your ears like a tiger, and if the angelic dove has, when casting its eyes on you, the look of a hyena; if the trim gentleman crossing the street is dressed in lecherous tatters; if the much-prized rose offered to you is a faded rag, less interesting than a sparrow; if the face of your wife is a furiously flaked piece of wood—your eyes, not God, made them like this.

When you die, the demons and the angels, both equally greedy, knowing you to be asleep, will appear disguised by the side of your bed and, stroking your brow, they will let you choose from whatever you preferred throughout your life. In a kind of stock-list they will show you, at first, the elemental things. If they show you the sun, the moon or the stars, you will see them in a painted crystal sphere, and you will believe that the sphere is the world; if they show you the sea or the mountains, you will see them in a stone and believe that stone to be the sea or the mountains; if they show you a horse, it will be a miniature horse, but you will imagine it to be a real one. The angels and the demons will divert your attention with pictures of flowers, candied fruit and chocolates, making you believe you are still a child; holding hands they will make a fireman's seat for you to sit on, and in this fashion they will carry you through the galleries, deep into the core of your life, to where your preferences lie. But be careful. If you choose more things from Hell than from Heaven, you may be sent to Heaven; on the other hand, if you choose more things from Heaven than from Hell, you run the risk of being sent to Hell, because your love for celestial things will show that you are merely avaricious.

The laws of Heaven and Hell are versatile. Whether you go to one place or the other may depend on an insignificant detail. I know people who because of a broken key or a wicker cage have gone to Hell, and others who because of a piece of newspaper or a cup of milk have gone to Heaven.

The Inextinguishable Race

IN THAT CITY all was perfect and small: the houses, the furniture, the working tools, the shops, the gardens. I tried to find out what highly progressive race of pygmies inhabited it. A bleary-eyed child gave me the following report:

"We are the ones who work: our parents, partly because of their selfishness, partly to please us, have implanted this style of living that is both agreeable and economical. While they sit at home, playing cards or a musical instrument, reading or talking, loving or hating (because they are passionate beings), we play at building, cleaning, wood-working, harvesting, selling. Our tools are built according to our size. With surprising ease we fulfill our daily obligations. I must confess that at first certain animals, especially the trained animals, did not obey us, because they knew we were children. But gradually, after a few tricks, they began to respect us. Our work is not difficult: just tiresome. Frequently we sweat like running horses. Sometimes we throw ourselves on the floor and say that we don't want to play any more (and we put grass or lumps of dirt in our mouths, or simply lick the tiles), but our tantrums last only a short while, 'a brief summer storm' as my cousin would say. Of course not everything is to our parents' advantage. They also suffer a few inconveniences; for instance, they are forced to enter their homes bent over, almost on all fours, because the doors and the rooms are so tiny. The word *tiny* is always on their lips. The quantity of food they receive, according to my greedy aunts, is minimal. The jugs and glasses from which they drink don't satisfy them and maybe that explains why lately there has been so much pilfering of pails and other containers. The clothes they wear fit tightly, because our machines are not made (nor will they be made) to produce larger sizes. Most of them, those who do not own several beds, sleep all hunched up. At night they shiver with cold, unless they cover themselves with a large quantity of blankets which, according to my poor father, are the size of handkerchiefs. Nowadays many people complain about the wedding cakes, which no one tastes out of politeness; about the wigs, which won't cover even the most moderate bald patches; about the cages which will fit only stuffed humming-birds. I suspect that, simply in order to show their sour dis-position, these same people almost never attend our ceremonies or dramatic performances or moving-pictures. I must say that they don't fit in the seats, and that the idea of sitting on the floor, in a public place, horrifies them. How-ever, some people of medium height, unscrupulous people (and every passing day there are more of these), occupy our places without us noticing it. We are credulous but not light-headed. It has taken us a long time to discover the impostors. Grown-ups, when they are small, very small, look a little like us; I mean, when we are tired. Their faces are lined with wrinkles, they have bags under their eyes, they speak in vague tones, mingling several languages. Once I was mistaken for one of these creatures: I don't even want to think of that day. Now the impostors are discovered with greater ease. We are on our guard, ready to expel them from our circle. We are happy. At least, I think we are happy.

"We are haunted, it is true, by certain misgivings: we have

heard the rumour that, because of us, people don't reach normal proportions when they grow up. I mean the inordinate proportions that characterize adults. Some have the height of a ten-year-old child; others, more fortunate, that of a seven-year-old. They pretend to be children and they don't understand that not just anyone who lacks a few inches can be a child. We, on the other hand, according to the latest statistics, diminish in height without growing weaker, without losing our identity, without trying to deceive anyone.

"This pleases us, but it also gives us cause for concern. My brother has already complained that his carpentry tools are too heavy for him. A friend has told me that her embroidering needle seems to her as large as a sword. I myself find the wielding of an axe a rather difficult task.

"We are not seriously concerned with the danger of our parents occupying the place they have left us—this is something we shall never allow, because, rather than hand over our machines, we will destroy them, we will destroy our electrical plants, our fresh water reserves. We are concerned with our future. We are concerned with the future of our race.

"However, it is true that some of us are convinced of this: that as we grow smaller, throughout the years, our vision of the world will become more and more intimate, that is to say, more and more human."

Translated by Alberto Manguel

The Stolen Party

LILIANA HEKER

In PARALYSING ARGENTINA *for over ten years, the generals also abolished several generations of writers, because it is almost impossible to write while your next-door neighbours are being dragged away screaming. However, in the midst of this chaos, one literary magazine survived almost miraculously, without having to change either its voice or its subject matter. The magazine was* El Ornitorrinco (The Platypus), *formerly known as* El Escarabajo de Oro (The Gold Bug), *and its motto was a line by Oscar Wilde: "One must always be a little improbable." Although directed by the short-story writer and playwright Abelardo Castillo, the thrust of the magazine depended on the editor-in-chief Liliana Heker. She had published her first book of short stories in her teens,* Los que vieron la zarza (Those Who Beheld the Burning Bush), *a collection that is still one of the best to have appeared in Argentina since the 1960s. In the pages of the magazine, Liliana Heker conducted a polemic with Julio Cortázar, who had chosen to live in Paris, on the role of the writer in a tortured society. Cortázar defended his position as political writer in exile, while Liliana Heker argued (echoing Nadine Gordimer's position in South Africa) that "to be heard, we must shout from within."*

As soon as she arrived she went straight to the kitchen to see if the monkey was there. It was: what a relief! She wouldn't have liked to admit that her mother had been right. *Monkeys at a birthday?* her mother had sneered. *Get away with you, believing any nonsense you're told!* She was cross, but not because of the monkey, the girl thought; it's just because of the party.

"I don't like you going," she told her. "It's a rich people's party."

"Rich people go to Heaven too," said the girl, who studied religion at school.

"Get away with Heaven," said the mother. "The problem with you, young lady, is that you like to fart higher than your ass."

The girl didn't approve of the way her mother spoke. She was barely nine, and one of the best in her class.

"I'm going because I've been invited," she said. "And I've been invited because Luciana is my friend. So there."

"Ah yes, your friend," her mother grumbled. She paused. "Listen, Rosaura," she said at last. "That one's not your friend. You know what you are to them? The maid's daughter, that's what."

Rosaura blinked hard: she wasn't going to cry. Then she yelled: "Shut up! You know nothing about being friends!"

Every afternoon she used to go to Luciana's house and they would both finish their homework while Rosaura's mother did the cleaning. They had their tea in the kitchen and they told each other secrets. Rosaura loved everything in the big house, and she also loved the people who lived there.

"I'm going because it will be the most lovely party in the whole world, Luciana told me it would. There will be a magician, and he will bring a monkey and everything."

The mother swung around to take a good look at her child, and pompously put her hands on her hips.

"Monkeys at a birthday?" she said. "Get away with you, believing any nonsense you're told!"

Rosaura was deeply offended. She thought it unfair of her mother to accuse other people of being liars simply because they were rich. Rosaura too wanted to be rich, of course. If one day she managed to live in a beautiful palace, would her mother stop loving her? She felt very sad. She wanted to go to that party more than anything else in the world.

"I'll die if I don't go," she whispered, almost without moving her lips.

And she wasn't sure whether she had been heard, but on the morning of the party she discovered that her mother had starched her Christmas dress. And in the afternoon, after washing her hair, her mother rinsed it in apple vinegar so that it would be all nice and shiny. Before going out, Rosaura admired herself in the mirror, with her white dress and glossy hair, and thought she looked terribly pretty.

Señora Ines also seemed to notice. As soon as she saw her, she said:

"How lovely you look today, Rosaura."

Rosaura gave her starched skirt a slight toss with her hands and walked into the party with a firm step. She said hello to Luciana and asked about the monkey. Luciana put on a secretive look and whispered into Rosaura's ear: "He's in the kitchen. But don't tell anyone, because it's a surprise."

Rosaura wanted to make sure. Carefully she entered the kitchen and there she saw it: deep in thought, inside its cage. It looked so funny that the girl stood there for a while, watching it, and later, every so often, she would slip out of the party unseen and go and admire it. Rosaura was the only one allowed into the kitchen. Señora Ines had said: "You yes, but not the others, they're much too boisterous, they might break something." Rosaura had never broken anything. She even managed the jug of orange juice, carrying it from the kitchen into the dining-room. She held it carefully and didn't spill a single drop. And Señora Ines had said: "Are you sure you can manage a jug as big as that?" Of course she could manage. She wasn't a butterfingers, like the others. Like that blonde girl with the bow in her hair. As soon as she saw Rosaura, the girl with the bow had said:

"And you? Who are you?"

"I'm a friend of Luciana," said Rosaura.

"No," said the girl with the bow, "you are not a friend of Luciana because I'm her cousin and I know all her friends. And I don't know you."

"So what," said Rosaura. "I come here every afternoon with my mother and we do our homework together."

"You and your mother do your homework together?" asked the girl, laughing.

"I and Luciana do our homework together," said Rosaura, very seriously.

The girl with the bow shrugged her shoulders.

"That's not being friends," she said. "Do you go to school together?"

"No."

"So where do you know her from?" said the girl, getting impatient.

Rosaura remembered her mother's words perfectly. She took a deep breath.

"I'm the daughter of the employee," she said.

Her mother had said very clearly: "If someone asks, you say you're the daughter of the employee; that's all." She also told her to add: "And proud of it." But Rosaura thought that never in her life would she dare say something of the sort.

"What employee?" said the girl with the bow. "Employee in a shop?"

"No," said Rosaura angrily. "My mother doesn't sell anything in any shop, so there."

"So how come she's an employee?" said the girl with the bow.

Just then Señora Ines arrived saying *shh shh*, and asked Rosaura if she wouldn't mind helping serve out the hot-dogs, as she knew the house so much better than the others.

"See?" said Rosaura to the girl with the bow, and when no one was looking she kicked her in the shin.

Apart from the girl with the bow, all the others were delightful. The one she liked best was Luciana, with her golden birthday crown; and then the boys. Rosaura won the sack race, and nobody managed to catch her when they played tag. When they split into two teams to play charades, all the boys wanted her for their side. Rosaura felt she had never been so happy in all her life.

But the best was still to come. The best came after Luciana blew out the candles. First the cake. Señora Ines had asked her to help pass the cake around, and Rosaura had enjoyed the task immensely, because everyone called out to her, shouting "Me, me!" Rosaura remembered a story in which there was a queen who had the power of life or death over her subjects. She had always loved that, having the power of life or death. To Luciana and the boys she gave the largest pieces, and to the girl with the bow she gave a slice so thin one could see through it.

After the cake came the magician, tall and bony, with a fine red cape. A true magician: he could untie handkerchiefs by blowing on them and make a chain with links that had no openings. He could guess what cards were pulled out from a pack, and the monkey was his assistant. He called the monkey "partner." "Let's see here, partner," he would say, "Turn over a card." And, "Don't run away, partner: time to work now."

The final trick was wonderful. One of the children had to hold the monkey in his arms and the magician said he would make him disappear.

"What, the boy?" they all shouted.

"No, the monkey!" shouted back the magician.

Rosaura thought that this was truly the most amusing party in the whole world.

The magician asked a small fat boy to come and help, but the small fat boy got frightened almost at once and dropped the monkey on the floor. The magician picked him up carefully, whispered something in his ear, and the monkey nodded almost as if he understood.

"You mustn't be so unmanly, my friend," the magician said to the fat boy.

"What's unmanly?" said the fat boy.

The magician turned around as if to look for spies.

"A sissy," said the magician. "Go sit down."

Then he stared at all the faces, one by one. Rosaura felt her heart tremble.

"You, with the Spanish eyes," said the magician. And everyone saw that he was pointing at her.

She wasn't afraid. Neither holding the monkey, nor when the magician made him vanish; not even when, at the end, the magician flung his red cape over Rosaura's head and uttered a few magic words . . . and the monkey reappeared, chattering happily, in her arms. The children clapped furiously. And before Rosaura returned to her seat, the magician said:

"Thank you very much, my little countess."

She was so pleased with the compliment that a while later, when her mother came to fetch her, that was the first thing she told her.

"I helped the magician and he said to me, 'Thank you very much, my little countess.'"

It was strange because up to then Rosaura had thought that she was angry with her mother. All along Rosaura had imagined that she would say to her: "See that the monkey wasn't a lie?" But instead she was so thrilled that she told her mother all about the wonderful magician.

Her mother tapped her on the head and said: "So now we're a countess!"

But one could see that she was beaming.

And now they both stood in the entrance, because a moment ago Señora Ines, smiling, had said: "Please wait here a second."

Her mother suddenly seemed worried.

"What is it?" she asked Rosaura.

"What is what?" said Rosaura. "It's nothing; she just wants to get the presents for those who are leaving, see?"

She pointed at the fat boy and at a girl with pigtails who were also waiting there, next to their mothers. And she explained about the presents. She knew, because she had been watching those who left before her. When one of the girls was about to leave, Señora Ines would give her a bracelet. When a boy left, Señora Ines gave him a yo-yo. Rosaura preferred the yo-yo because it sparkled, but she didn't mention that to her mother. Her mother might have said: "So why don't you ask for one, you blockhead?" That's what her mother was like. Rosaura didn't feel like explaining that she'd be horribly ashamed to be the odd one out. Instead she said:

"I was the best-behaved at the party."

And she said no more because Señora Ines came out into the hall with two bags, one pink and one blue.

First she went up to the fat boy, gave him a yo-yo out of the blue bag, and the fat boy left with his mother. Then she went up to the girl and gave her a bracelet out of the pink bag, and the girl with the pigtails left as well.

Finally she came up to Rosaura and her mother. She had a big smile on her face and Rosaura liked that. Señora Ines looked down at her, then looked up at her mother, and then said something that made Rosaura proud:

"What a marvellous daughter you have, Herminia."

For an instant, Rosaura thought that she'd give her two presents: the bracelet and the yo-yo. Señora Ines bent down as if about to look for something. Rosaura also leaned forward, stretching out her arm. But she never completed the movement.

Señora Ines didn't look in the pink bag. Nor did she look in the blue bag. Instead she rummaged in her purse. In her hand appeared two bills.

"You really and truly earned this," she said handing them over. "Thank you for all your help, my pet."

Rosaura felt her arms stiffen, stick close to her body, and then she noticed her mother's hand on her shoulder. Instinctively she pressed herself against her mother's body. That was all. Except her eyes. Rosaura's eyes had a cold, clear look that fixed itself on Señora Ines's face.

Señora Ines, motionless, stood there with her hand outstretched. As if she didn't dare draw it back. As if the slightest change might shatter an infinitely delicate balance.

Translated by Alberto Manguel

It's the Fault of
the Tlaxcaltecas

ELENA GARRO

MEXICO'S DUAL HERITAGE, *Spanish and Indian, was defined
by the poet Octavio Paz in his now classical essay, "El labe-
rinto de la soledad" ("The Labyrinth of Solitude"), published
in 1950. But it was Elena Garro (who later married and then
divorced Paz) who first explored the theme in her magical
short plays, written and performed in the 1940s. Perhaps the
most famous one of these is* Un hogar sólido (A Solid Home),
*a vision of the afterworld in which the dead members of a
family wait patiently for new arrivals, combining in their be-
liefs Catholic superstitions and an Indian sense of the land's
divinity. Garro's hallucinatory vision of the world (and the
hereafter) is further explored in her novel* Recuerdos del Porvenir (Recollections of Things to Come), *written in 1963,
and in her book of short stories,* La semana de colores
(A Week in Colours), *published a year later.*

    *The Cuban novelist Severo Sarduy told me of a visit to
Elena Garro when she was still married to Octavio Paz. Paz
was working on the theory that the theme of incest, one of the
ground themes in Mexican literature, was inherited from the
Indians. He had been talking about this for several hours
when at last Garro stopped him. "Instead of all this theory,"
she said, "why don't you try it out for once? I'll call your
sister, and we'll all three head for the bedroom." With a hurt
look on his face, Paz got up and left. "Now he'll never know if
it's in his blood, will he?" Elena Garro asked Sarduy.*

NACHA HEARD A knocking on the kitchen door and stood still. When the knocking was repeated she opened cautiously and peered into the night. Señora Laura was there, with her white suit scorched and stained with dirt and blood.

"Señora . . ." she whispered.

They came into the kitchen.

"Nacha, get me some coffee. I'm cold. . . ."

"Señora, the Señor. . . . The Señor will kill you. We'd given you up for dead."

"Dead?"

Laura stared sadly at the white kitchen tiles, propped her feet up on a chair, hugged her knees and remained thoughtful. Nacha put the water on for coffee and looked at her mistress from the corners of her eyes; she could not think of anything to say. The Señora pressed her head against her knees.

"You know what, Nacha? It's the fault of the Tlaxcaltecas."

Nacha made no answer. Instead she watched the water in the kettle. Outside the night effaced the garden roses and darkened the fig trees. Behind the branches shone the lit windows of the neighbouring houses. The kitchen seemed cut off from the rest of the world by an invisible melancholy wall.

"Don't you agree, Nacha?"

"Yes, Señora."

"I'm just like them: unfaithful . . ." Laura said sadly. The cook crossed her arms waiting for the water to heat up.

"And what about you, Nachita, are you unfaithful?"

She looked at her hopefully. If Nacha shared with her the quality of unfaithfulness, she'd understand. And Laura needed someone to understand her tonight.

Nacha thought for a moment, turned to watch the water that was just beginning to bubble noisily, and poured it over the coffee. The warm smell made her feel comfortable with her mistress.

"Yes, I too am unfaithful, Señora Laura."

Pleased, she poured coffee into a small white cup, put in two lumps of sugar, and set it on the table in front of her mistress, who, lost in thought, took a few sips.

"You know what, Nachita? Now I know why we had so many mishaps on that famous trip to Guanajuato. At Mil Cumbres we ran out of gas. Margarita got frightened because it was getting dark. A truck driver had to give us a little gas to reach Morella. In Cuitzeo, crossing the white bridge, the car suddenly stopped again. Margarita got cross with me: you know she's frightened of lonely roads and Indian eyes. When a tourist bus came along she went into town to find a mechanic and I sat there in the car, in the middle of the white bridge across the dry lake of white stone slabs. The light was very bright, and the bridge, the slabs, and the car seemed to float in it. The light broke into a thousand pieces that quickly turned into clouds of little dots and began to spin until it stopped, fixed as in a portrait. Time had gone full circle, like a postcard you turn over to see what is written on the back. And there, on Lake Cuitzeo, I became a child again. You know, light makes these things happen when the sun turns white and you stand alone in the very centre of the blaze. Your thoughts turn to sand; vertigo overcomes you. I looked down at my white dress, and then I heard his footsteps. I was not in the least surprised. I lifted my eyes and saw him coming towards me. Then I remembered my unfaithfulness; I felt afraid and tried to run. But time closed up around me, it became solid and deadly, and I simply couldn't move from my seat. "One day you'll find yourself face to face with your sins, turned into stones as unmoveable as these," they told me as a child, pointing to the image of a god, I don't remember which. We forget everything, don't we, Nachita? But not for long. As a child the words the adults spoke felt like stones, liquid crystal stones. The stones became hard at the end of every word, solidified in time. Weren't the words of your elders always like that?"

Nacha thought for a moment, then nodded with conviction.

"So they were, Señora Laurita."

"The terrible thing, I discovered then, is that anything unbelievable is true. And there he was, walking towards me along the edge of the bridge, his skin burnt by the sun, his misery weighing heavily on his naked shoulders. His footsteps crackled as if he were walking in dry leaves; his eyes were shining brightly. Their black sparks reached me from a distance and I saw his black hair blow in the very white light. Before I could even try to avoid him, he was there—right in front of my eyes. He stopped, held on to the door of the car, and stared at me. He had a cut on his left hand, his hair was full of dust, and from a wound on his shoulder oozed blood so red it seemed almost black. He said nothing, but I knew he was again on the run, defeated. He tried to ask me to die, and at the same time told me that my death would mean his own. He was badly hurt, and in search of me. 'It's the fault of the Tlaxcaltecas,' I said. He turned to look at the sky, and then he let his eyes fall once again on me.

" 'How are you now? How have you been?' he asked in a deep voice.

"I couldn't tell him I had got married because I knew I was married to *him*. There are things that can't be said, you know, Nachita?

" 'And the others?' I asked him.

" 'Those who escaped alive are in the same shape I am.'

"I realized that each word hurt his tongue; I said no more, thinking of shameful betrayal.

" 'You know I was afraid; that's why I was unfaithful. . . .'

" 'I know,' he said, and lowered his head.

"He has known me ever since I was a girl, Nacha. His father and my father were brothers. He always loved me—at least he said he did and we all believed him. So there on the bridge I felt ashamed. Blood kept running down his chest. I took a handkerchief out of my purse and without saying a word I began wiping the blood. I too have always loved him, Nachita, because he is everything I'm not. He's not afraid, he's not unfaithful. He took hold of my hand and looked at it.

" 'It's faded, bleached; it looks like one of their hands,' he said.

" 'It's been a while since I've been out in the sun.'

"He lowered his eyes and let go of my hand. We waited like that, in silence, listening to the blood running down his chest. He blamed me for nothing: he knows me. But the blood on his chest clung to my words and my body.

" 'My house?' I asked him.

" 'Let's go and see it.'

"He held me with his hot hand as he used to hold his medallion, and then I noticed he wasn't wearing it. 'He must have lost it during his flight,' I thought, and let myself be taken away. His footsteps crackled in the light of Cuitzeo as they had done on the bridge: dull and peaceful. We walked through the city that burned on the banks of the water. I closed my eyes. I've already told you, Nacha, I'm a coward. Maybe the smoke and dust brought tears to my eyes. I sat down on a stone.

" 'I can't walk any further!' And I covered my face with my hands.

" 'We're almost there,' he answered.

"He crouched down next to me and with his fingertips touched my white dress.

" 'If you don't want to see it now, we won't,' he said softly.

His black hair cast a shadow over me. He wasn't angry, only sad. Before, I would never have dared to kiss him, but I had learnt not to respect him; I put my arms around his neck and kissed him on the mouth.

" 'You've always been deep inside my heart,' he said.

"He lowered his head and stared at the ground covered with dry pebbles. With one he drew two parallel lines and followed them until they became one.

" 'You and me,' he said without lifting his eyes.

"Nachita, I was speechless.

" 'Soon Time will come to an end, and we'll truly be one. . . . That's why I set out to find you.'

"I had forgotten, Nachita; at the end of Time, we would both burn into one another, we would enter real Time, transformed into each other. As he spoke, I stared up at him. Before, I was only able to hold his look when he made love to me, but now, as I told you, I've learnt not to respect a man's eyes. Nor did I want to see what was happening around me: I knew I had to run away. I remembered shouts, and then heard them again, piercing, flaming in the morning. I also heard the thud of stones and saw them fly over my head. He kneeled down in front of me and crossed his arms over my head to make a roof.

" 'This is the end,' I said.

" 'Yes,' he answered, his voice above mine. And I saw myself in his eyes and in his body. What would the end be like? Would it be a stag carrying me to a mountainside? Or a star, forcing me to write symbols in the sky? His voice carved bloodsigns on my breast and my white dress was striped like the skin of a red and white tiger.

" 'I'll come at night. Wait for me!' he said.

"He held his medallion and looked down at me.

" 'We were almost one,' he added. As he left I heard the shouts again and ran out under the hail of stones and lost my way until I reached the car on the bridge over Lake Cuitzeo.

" 'What happened? Are you hurt?' Margarita cried, touching the blood on my white dress. I also had blood on my lips and my hair was full of dirt.

"From another car, the Cuitzeo mechanic looked at me with dull eyes.

" 'Those savages! You can't leave a lady alone for a moment!' he said, jumping from the car to help me. At nightfall we reached Mexico City. Nacha, I couldn't believe how much it had changed! At midday the Indian warriors had still been there, and now there was not a trace of their passing. Not even rubble. We crossed the silent and sad district of Zocalo; of the other marketplace there was nothing. Nothing left! Margarita was watching me from the corner of her eye. When we reached the house you opened the door. Remember?"

Nacha nodded. It was true that barely two months ago the Señora and her mother-in-law had gone on a trip to Guanajuato. The night they came back, Josefina the maid, and she, Nacha, had noticed blood on the dress but had said nothing because the Señora Margarita had signalled them to keep quiet; she seemed worried. Later Josefina told Nacha that at the table the Señor had looked angrily at the Señora and had said:

"Why haven't you changed? Do you enjoy brooding over foul memories?"

Señora Margarita had told him what had happened at Cuitzeo Bridge and lifted her hand as if to say "Be quiet, have pity on her!" Señora Laurita didn't answer, passed a finger over her lips and smiled. The Señor began, once again, to speak about Our President.

"You know, the President's name is always on his lips," Josefina had said scornfully. How bored Señora Laurita must have been, always hearing him talk about the President and the official visits!

"How strange, Nachita. I had never noticed how Pablo bored me, until that night!" Laura added, suddenly confirming Nacha's thoughts.

The cook crossed her arms and nodded.

"As soon as I entered the house, the furniture, the crystal vases and the mirrors fell upon me and made me even sadder than I already was. 'How many years, how many days will I have to wait before my cousin comes to take me away?' I said to myself, and regretted my unfaithfulness. During dinner I noticed that Pablo spoke not with words but with letters. And I began counting them, staring at his thick mouth and his one dead eye. All at once he fell silent. You know how he suddenly forgets what he's saying. He sat there with his arms hanging down. 'This new husband of mine can't remember a thing,' I said. 'All he knows is common, everyday facts.' 'Your world is muddled and dark, Laura,' he answered, looking again at the stains on my dress. Poor Margarita became flustered and as we were having coffee she stood up to put on a record.

" 'To cheer you up!' she said, smiling, because she could see a quarrel brewing.

"We sat without saying a word. The house filled with sounds. I stared at Pablo. 'He looks like . . .' I dared not go any further; I was afraid he'd read my thoughts. But it's true he's very like him, Nacha. Both love water and cool houses. Both watch the sky in the evening, both have black hair and white teeth. But Pablo speaks in little jumps, gets angry for the slightest reason, and asks all the time 'What are you thinking about?' My cousin-husband neither does nor says these things."

"True! Very true! The Señor is a fool!" said Nacha with disgust.

Laura sighed and looked at her cook with relief. At least here was someone she could trust.

"At night, while Pablo was kissing me, I kept saying to myself 'At what time will he come to get me?' And I almost cried thinking of the blood on his shoulder. And I couldn't forget his arms crossed above my head to make a roof. I was frightened that Pablo would notice that my cousin had kissed me only a few hours earlier. But he noticed nothing. And if it hadn't been for Josefina, the fright she gave me in the morning, Pablo would not have known a thing!"

Nachita agreed. Josefina, with her taste for scandal, was to blame. Nacha had said to Josefina, "Shut up, shut up for God's sake! There's a good reason why they haven't heard us shouting." But no; Josefina came into the bedroom with the breakfast tray and blurted out what she should have kept to herself:

"Señora, last night a man was peeping through your bedroom window! Nacha and I screamed and screamed."

"We heard nothing. . . ." the Señor said in surprise.

"It was him. . . !" the Señora whispered foolishly.

"Who?" the Señor asked, looking at the Señora with murder in his eyes. (At least that was how Josefina described him afterwards.)

Frightened, the Señora put a hand on her mouth, and when the Señor kept on asking angrily, she answered:

"The Indian . . . the Indian who followed me from Cuitzeo to Mexico City."

That is how Josefina learned about the Indian, and told Nachita.

"We must call the police!" the Señor yelled back.

Josefina showed him the window through which the stranger had been peering and Señor Pablo examined it carefully; on the window-sill were traces of almost fresh blood.

"He's hurt," said Señor Pablo, concerned. He took a few steps through the room and stopped in front of his wife.

"It *was* an Indian, Señor," said Josefina, corroborating Laura's words.

Pablo saw the white dress thrown over a chair and picked it up violently.

"Can you tell me how these stains got here?"

The Señora stood speechless, staring at the dark patches on the front of her dress, and the Señor hit the chest of drawers with his fist, then slapped the Señora across the face. All this was seen and heard by Josefina.

"He's violent, his behaviour is as incoherent as his words. It's not my fault if he accepted his defeat and then forgot about it," Laura said, lifting the dregs of the coffee from the bottom of the cup with her finger. Seeing her do this, Nacha filled the cup again.

"Drink your coffee, Señora," she said, convinced by her mistress's talk. "After all, what was the Señor complaining about? Anybody would see that you, Señora Laurita, are not for him."

"I fell in love with Pablo on the road somewhere, in a flash; I thought then that he reminded me of someone I knew, someone I couldn't quite remember. Afterwards, sometimes, I would recapture that instant in which he seemed to turn into that someone. But that never happened. Immediately he became absurd again, with no memories, like an uninhabited body, repeating the gestures of every man in Mexico City. How could I not notice the deceit? When he gets angry, he forbids me to go out. How many times does he pick a fight in restaurants and cinemas? You know, Nachita. . . . My husband-cousin, now, never *ever* gets mad at his wife!"

Nacha knew her mistress was speaking the truth. That

morning, when Josefina ran in frightened, screaming "Wake up, Señora Margarita! The Señor is hitting the Señora!" she, Nacha, ran to get the Señor's mother.

The presence of his mother calmed Señor Pablo. And Señora Margarita seemed very surprised to hear about the Indian. She hadn't seen him; she had only seen the blood, like everyone else.

"Maybe you suffered a sunstroke, Laura, and your nose began to bleed. Remember, son, that the roof of the car was open," she said, without knowing what to say.

Señora Laura lay face down on the bed, locked in her thoughts, while her husband and his mother argued.

"You know, Nachita, what I was thinking this morning? What if he saw me, last night, while Pablo was kissing me? I felt like crying. I remembered that when a man and a woman really love each other and have no children, they are condemned to becoming a single being. That's what my uncle-father used to tell me, when I used to take him his water, and he would glance at the door behind which my husband-cousin and I slept. Everything he said was now happening. With my head on the pillow I heard Pablo and Margarita argue, and it all sounded so foolish. I'll go and get him, I said to myself. But where? Later, when you and Josefina came to my room to ask me about dinner, a thought struck me: at the Cafe Tacuba! I had never been there before, but I had heard it mentioned."

Nacha remembered her mistress, as if she saw her that very instant, her mistress putting on the white blood-stained dress, the same she wore now.

"For God's sake, Laura, don't put on that dress!" her mother-in-law had said. But Laura paid no attention. To hide the stains she pulled a white sweater over it, buttoned it up to the neck, and walked out without saying good-bye. But the worst was still to come. Or maybe the worst was to come now, in the kitchen, if Señora Margarita were to wake up.

"The Cafe Tacuba was empty. It's a dreary place. The waiter came to my table.

" 'What will you have?'

"I wasn't thirsty, but I had to ask for something.

" 'A *cocada*.'

"My cousin and I, we used to eat coconuts when we were little, Nacha. In the cafe a clock was ticking away. 'All over the city clocks are ticking away time,' I said to myself as I was eating. 'It must be wasting itself away, slowly. When only a transparent sheet of time remains, he will arrive, and the two drawn lines will be one, and I will live forever in his heart.'

" 'How late is it?' I asked the waiter.

" 'Twelve o'clock.'

" 'Pablo arrives at one,' I said to myself. 'If I get a taxi to take me through the shortcut, I can still wait a while.' But I didn't wait, I went out into the street. The sun was silvery, beating on my head. My thoughts turned to luminous dust and suddenly there was no past, no present, no future. On the pavement stood my cousin, blocking my way. He stared at me with sad eyes for a long while.

" 'What are you doing?' he asked me in his deep voice.

" 'I was waiting for you.'

"He stood still, like a panther. I saw his black hair and the red wound on his shoulder.

" 'Weren't you afraid to come out here on your own?' he asked.

"Stones and voices screamed past our ears, and I felt something burn behind my back.

" 'Don't look!' he said. He knelt down and with his fingers he put out the fire on my dress. It had burst into flames.

" 'Get me out of here!' I yelled with all my strength. All of a sudden, I remembered standing at the door of my father's house, and the house was burning, and my father and brothers all dead. I saw the memory frozen in his eyes, as he knelt before me putting out the fire on my dress. I let myself fall into his arms. With his hot hand he covered my eyes.

" 'This is the end of the world!' I said, my eyes beneath his hand.

" 'Don't look!'

"He held me against his heart. I heard it beat like thunder in the mountains. How long before Time ended and I could hear it forever? My tears cooled his hand burning with the city. Screams and stones were all around us, but I felt safe against his chest.

" 'Sleep with me. . . ,' he said very softly.

" 'Did you see me last night?' I asked.

" 'I saw you. . . ,' he said unhappily.

"We fell asleep in the morning light, in the heat of the fire. When we woke up, he leaped to his feet and grabbed his medallion.

" 'Hide somewhere until dawn. I'll come and get you.'

"He ran off on bare feet. . . . And I ran away, Nacha, again, because, all alone, I felt afraid."

" 'Lady, you feel all right?'

"A voice like Pablo's spoke to me in the street.

" 'Who do you think you're talking to? Leave me alone!'

"I got into a taxi and it brought me home through the bypass. And I arrived. . . ."

Nacha remembered the arrival; she had opened the door herself. And she had also broken the news to the Señora. (Josefina came down later, stumbling down the stairs.)

"Señora, the Señor and the Señora Margarita have gone to the police!"

Laura stood staring, saying nothing.

"Where were you, Señora?"

"I went to the Cafe Tacuba."

"But that was two days ago!"

Josefina brought in the paper, *Ultimas Noticias*. . . . She had been to school for a time so she could read the headlines: "Señora Aldama still missing," "It is feared the sinister Indian who followed her from Cuitzeo is a sadist," "Police are searching for her in Michoacan and Guanajuato." Laura snatched the paper from Josefina's hands and tore it up in fury. Then she went to her room. Nacha and Josefina followed her; it was best not to leave her alone. They saw her throw herself on the bed and dream with her eyes wide open. The same thought struck both women, and they voiced it later, in the kitchen. "I think Señora Laurita is in love." But when the Señor arrived they were still in her room.

"Laura!" the Señor called out. He ran to the bed and took her in his arms. "My sweetheart!" he wept.

Señora Laurita seemed to mellow for a moment.

"Señor!" Josefina cried. "The Señora's dress is scorched all over!"

Nacha looked at her disapprovingly. The Señor inspected the dress and then his wife's feet.

"It's true. Even the soles of your shoes are burnt. My love, where were you? What happened?"

"At the Cafe Tacuba," the Señora answered calmly.

Señora Margarita wrung her hands and walked up to her daughter-in-law.

"We know you were there the day before yesterday, and that you ate a *cocada*. And then?"

"Then I took a taxi and came home through the bypass."

Nacha looked down. Josefina opened her mouth as if to say something. Señora Margarita bit her lips. Pablo took his wife by the shoulders and shook her violently.

"Stop playing the fool! Where were you these two days? Why is your dress all burnt?"

"Burnt? But he . . ." Señora Laura let the words escape.

"He? That filthy Indian?" Pablo shook her again with anger.

"I met him as I left the Cafe Tacuba. . . ." Señora Laura wept in fright.

"I never thought you'd stoop to that!" said the Señor and dropped her on the bed.

"Tell us who he is," Señora Margarita asked, softening her voice.

"Isn't it true, Nachita, that I couldn't tell them he was my husband?" Laura said, begging her cook's approval.

Nacha agreed with her mistress's discretion and remembered that at midday, worried about Laura's situation, she had said:

"Maybe the Cuitzeo Indian is a witch doctor."

But Señora Margarita had turned on her with burning eyes and answered, almost screaming:

"A witch doctor? You mean a murderer!"

After that, for many days, Señora Laurita was not allowed out. The Señor ordered that the windows and doors of the house be put under surveillance. The maids would frequently enter their mistress's room to see how she was. Nacha refused to comment on what had happened or say what had surprised her. But who could make Josefina hold her tongue?

"Señora, at dawn the Indian was again at the window," she announced as she brought in the breakfast tray.

The Señora leapt to the window and found once again the trace of fresh blood. The Señora began to cry.

"Poor thing . . . poor thing . . ." she said, sobbing.

That afternoon the Señor came back with the doctor. After that, the doctor came to see her every evening.

"He would ask me about my childhood, about my father and mother. But I didn't know which childhood he meant, which father, which mother. So I would talk to him about the Conquest of Mexico. You do understand me, don't you?" Laura said, her eyes on the yellow saucepan.

"Yes, Señora . . ." And Nachita peered into the garden through the window panes. Night was so tiresome, not being able to see anything among the shadows! She thought of the Señor, seated at the table with a worried look, barely touching his dinner.

"Mother, Laura asked the doctor to bring her Bernal Diaz del Castillo's *History of the Conquest*; she says that's all she cares about."

Señora Margarita dropped her fork.

"Poor son! Your wife is losing her mind!"

"All she can talk about is the fall of the Great Tenochtitlan," Pablo added, his head bowed.

Then the doctor, Señora Margarita and Pablo agreed that Laura was suffering from nervous depression, and that being locked up did her no good; that it was time for her to face the world again, and her responsibilities. After that day, the Señor would send the car around for his wife to take drives around Chapultepec Park. She would leave the house in the company of her mother-in-law, and the chauffeur was under strict orders to watch them both closely. But the fresh air did her no good, and Nacha and Josefina would see her come back each time more exhausted. As soon as she entered the house she would plunge into Bernal Diaz; only then would her face light up again.

One morning Señora Margarita returned alone and distraught.

"The madwoman's escaped!" she shouted as she entered the house.

"You see, Nacha, in Chapultepec Park I sat down on the same bench as usual and said to myself, 'He won't forgive me. A man can forgive one, two, three, four betrayals, but not

constant unfaithfulness, no.' The thought made me unhappy. As it was so hot, Margarita bought herself a vanilla
ice-cream and sat in the car. I saw that she was as bored with
me as I was bored with her. I don't like being watched over,
and I tried to look at other things so that I wouldn't see her
eating her ice-cream and watching me. I saw the grey moss
hanging from the trees, and, God knows why, the morning
turned as sad as the trees. 'They have seen the same things I
have seen,' I said to myself. The lonely hours drifted down
the empty sidewalk. I felt like that myself: alone, on the empty
road. My cousin had seen my everlasting unfaithfulness
through the window, and had left me on that sidewalk made
of non-existent things. I remembered the smell of the corn
leaves and the crackling sound of his footsteps. He walked
like that, with the rhythm of the dead leaves thrown by the
February wind on the stones. Before, I didn't even need to
turn my head to know that he was there, his eyes on my back
before he appeared in front of me. I let my thoughts run on
sadly. Suddenly I heard the sun change place and the dead
leaves move. His breath fell on my shoulders: I saw his naked
feet. He had a long scratch down his knee. I raised my eyes
and found myself under his. For a long moment we said
nothing. Out of a new respect for him I waited for his first
words.

" 'What are you doing?' he said.

"I saw him motionless, and sadder than before.

" 'The last day will soon come. . . .'

"His voice seemed to spring from the depths of Time. His
shoulder was still bleeding. I was filled with shame. I lowered
my eyes, opened my purse and drew out a handkerchief to
clean his chest. Then I put it away. He stood there, watching
me.

" 'Let's go to Tacuba. . . .'

"He took my hand and we left, making our way through

the people who now were shouting and complaining. Many corpses were floating in the water of the ditches. There were women sitting on the grass, watching them float by. The plague was rising from everywhere and children ran, here and there, looking for their parents. I looked at it all without wanting to see. My cousin-husband sat me under a broken tree. He knelt down and looked keenly around. Then he faced me.

" 'I know you're unfaithful, but that you care for me. Good goes with bad.'

"The children's screams barely let me hear what he was saying. They came from far away, but they were so loud that they broke into the very light of· day. It sounded as if they were crying out for the last time.

" 'It's the children,' he said.

" 'It's the end of the world,' I recited, because no other thought came to mind.

"He covered my ears with his hands and then drew me against his breast.

" 'I met you when you were unfaithful and I loved you.'

" 'You were born under an unlucky star,' I said to him.

"I hugged him. My cousin-husband closed his eyes to stop the tears. We lay down on the broken branches. The shouts of the warriors, the hissing stones and the children's cries reached us even there.

" 'Time is running out . . .' my cousin-husband sighed.

"Through a crack in a wall the women who did not want to die on that day were trying to escape. The men fell in rows, one after the other, as if they were holding hands, as if a single blow felled them all together. Some died letting out such loud screams that they kept on echoing long after their deaths.

"Soon it would be time for us to become one for ever. My cousin stood up, gathered some branches and made me a hut.

" 'Wait for me here.'

"He stared at me, and then left to join the fight with the others. I stayed behind, all hunched up. I didn't want to see the people running, I didn't want to be tempted into running away myself, nor did I want to see the dead floating in the water. I began counting the tiny fruit hanging from the cut branches; they were dry, and when you touched them the red skin would fall off. I don't know why, they seemed a bad omen, and I looked instead at the sky which was beginning to grow dark. First it turned brownish, then it began to take on the colour of the drowned men in the ditches. I sat motionless remembering the colours of other evenings. But the sky kept on growing darker, swelling up, as if it were about to burst, and I knew Time had come to an end. If my cousin did not return, what would become of me? I stopped caring for him and ran out as fast as I could, pursued by my fear. 'When he comes back and looks for me. . . .' I didn't have time to finish my thought because I suddenly found myself in the dusk of Mexico City. 'Margarita must have finished her vanilla ice-cream and Pablo must be furious. . . .' I thought. A taxi brought me along the bypass. You know what, Nachita? The bypass turned into a ditch full of bodies. . . . That's why I was so sad when I got back. Nachita, don't tell the Señor that I spent the afternoon with my real husband."

Nachita put her hands on her lilac skirt.

"Señor Pablo left for Acapulco ten days ago. He was ever so thin after the weeks of searching," Nachita explained with satisfaction.

Laura sighed with relief.

"Señora Margarita is upstairs," Nacha added, turning her eyes towards the kitchen ceiling.

Laura hugged her knees and stared out of the window at the roses fading in the shadows, and at the neighbouring lights slowly being switched off.

Nachita put salt on the back of her hand and licked it hungrily.

"So many coyotes! The pack is all excited," she said, her mouth full of salt.

Laura listened for a few minutes.

"Dumb animals, you should have seen them this afternoon," she said.

"As long as they don't stand in the way of the Señor," Nacha said, unafraid.

"He was never afraid of them. Why should he be afraid now?" Laura asked with pride.

Nacha approached her mistress, so that distance would not disturb the sudden intimacy.

"They're worse than the Tlaxcaltecas," she said in a low voice. And she helped herself to more salt, licking it slowly with the tip of her tongue. Laura felt worried, listening to the coyotes filling the night. It was Nacha who saw him arrive and opened the window.

"Señora. . . . He's come to get you. . . ."

Afterwards, when Laura had left for good, Nacha cleaned the blood off the window-sill and shooed away the coyotes who were trying to invade her time, her century which was vanishing that very instant. Nacha looked around to see if all was tidy. She washed the coffee cup, threw away the lipstick-stained cigarette butts, put away the coffee pot and turned off the light, leaving no trace of her mistress's passing.

"I must say that Señora Laurita was not of this time, nor was she meant for the Señor," she explained that morning as she carried Señora Margarita her breakfast.

"I'm not comfortable here. I'll look for another place," she said to Josefina. And when the maid turned her back, Nacha left without asking for her wages.

Translated by Alberto Manguel

Tigrela

LYGIA FAGUNDES TELLES

THE MODERN BRAZILIAN short story begins with Machado de Assis, who at the turn of the century created an absurdist world reminiscent of Kafka's. Though Lygia Fagundes Telles follows this tradition in "Tigrela," most of her other work barely hints at the darker side of dreams, glimpsed behind the rustling of social conventions. She began writing very young and later complained that the youth of her time "lived in ignorance, tied down by unquestioned laws. We live in shame and fear." Her celebrated novel As Meninas *(translated into English as* The Girl in the Photograph) *uses a thriller device —a mysterious phone call—to explore these feelings of "ignorance, shame and fear" in three young girls. "Tigrela" is a more subtle study of a woman's psyche, exploring a metaphor of what Fagundes Telles calls "the green jungles inside us, the foliage moist with blood."*

I BUMPED INTO Romana by chance, in a café. She was half drunk but far down at the bottom of her transparent drunkenness I sensed a thick sediment which stirred up quickly when she became serious. Then her mouth curved downward, heavy; her expression became fugitive. Twice she squeezed my hand, I need you, she said. But immediately afterward she didn't need me any more and her fear turned to indifference, almost scorn, with a certain torpidity thickening her lips. When she laughed she was an adolescent again, the best of our class without a doubt. Without a danger. She had been beautiful and still was, but her now-corrupted beauty was sad even when she was happy. She told me she had separated from her fifth husband and was living with a small tiger in a penthouse.

With a tiger, Romana? She laughed. She'd had a boy-friend who had travelled through Asia and he had brought back Tigrela with the baggage, in a little basket. She was teeny-tiny and had to be raised on a bottle. She had grown to be just a little bigger than a cat, the kind with tawny fur and toast-coloured stripes, golden eyes. Two-thirds tiger and one-third woman, she's gotten more and more human and now . . . In the beginning it was funny, she imitated me so much, and I started imitating her, too, and we ended up getting so involved with each other that I don't remember if it was she who taught me to look at myself slit-eyed in the mirror. Or if she learned from me to stretch out on the floor and rest her head on her arms to listen to music, she's so harmonious. So clean, said Romana, dropping an ice cube into the glass. Her fur is this colour, she added, swirling the whisky. With the tips of her fingers she gathered up the thin blade of ice that was melting in the bottom of the glass. She crunched it between her teeth. The sound made me remember that she used to chew ice-cream. This Tigrela liked whisky but she knew how to drink, she had self-control, only once did she go so far as to get really smashed. And Romana laughed as she recalled the animal turning somersaults, rolling across the furniture until she jumped up onto the chandelier and perched there swinging back and forth, Romana said weakly imitating the movement of a pendulum. She crashed down with one half of the chandelier onto the big cushion, where we danced a tango together, it was atrocious. Afterwards she got depressed and at such times she loses her temper, she almost levelled the garden, tore up my bathrobe, broke things. In the end she wanted to throw herself off the parapet of the terrace, just exactly like a person. Exactly, repeated Romana looking for the watch on my wrist. She appealed to a man who passed by alongside our table, the time, the time! When she learned that it was almost midnight she lowered her eyes in sober calculation. She remained silent; I waited. When she began talking again, she seemed to me like an excited player hiding her strategy behind an artificial voice: I had steel railings attached to the wall, all around, if she wants, she can climb this railing easily, of course. But I know she'd only attempt suicide if drunk, and so I can just close the door that leads to the terrace. She's always so sober, she went on, lowering her voice; her face darkened. What is it, Romana? I asked, touching her hand. It was icy. She fixed her eyes on me astutely. She was thinking of something else when she told me that at sunset, when the light slanted over the top of the building, the shadow of the railing was projected halfway across the living room rug, and if Tigrela was sleeping on the big cushion, the pattern cast over her fur by the shadow was beautiful, like a net.

She stirred the ice cube in her glass of whisky with her index finger. On this finger she wore a square-cut emerald, like queens do. But wasn't it extraordinary, really. The limited space of the apartment conditioned the growth of an Asiatic tiger through the magic wisdom of adaptation, she's really nothing more than an overgrown tabby, as though she intuited the need to restrict herself; no bigger than a big cat. I alone realize that she's grown, I'm the only one who notices that she's taking up more space even though she's still the same size. Lately there's hardly room for us both, one of us will really have to . . . She interrupted herself to light a small cigarillo, the flame flickering in her trembling hand. She sleeps with me but when she's in a huff she goes to sleep on the big cushion, on her back, stiff as a sphinx.

There must have been so many problems, what about the neighbours? I asked. Romana stiffened the finger which whirled the ice. There aren't any neighbours, one apartment per floor in a very tall building, all white, Mediterranean style, you should see how well Tigrela matches the apartment. I travelled through Persia, you know, don't you? And I brought back fabrics, rugs, she adores this velvet comfort, she's so sensitive to the touch of things, to smells. When she wakes up restless, I light the incense; the perfume calms her. I turn on the record player. And then she stretches herself all over and sleeps, I suspect she sees better with her eyes closed, like dragons do. I had some trouble convincing Aninha that she was merely a well-developed cat, Aninha is the maid. But now everything's fine, the two of them keep a certain distance, but respect each other, the important thing is this respect. She accepted Aninha, who is old and ugly, but she almost attacked the former maid, a young girl. As long as this girl was with me, Tigrela practically didn't come out of the garden, hidden among the foliage, her eyes slits, her fingernails dug into the ground.

Fingernails, I began and forgot what I was going to say next. The emerald slid sideways like an unsupported head and clinked against the glass, the finger too thin for the ring. The sound of the stone hitting the glass roused Romana, momentarily apathetic. She lifted her head and gazed vacantly at the ·

full tables, such noise, eh? I suggested we leave, but instead of the bill she called for another whisky, don't worry, I'm used to it, she said and breathed deeply. She straightened her body. Tigrela liked jewels and Bach, yes, Bach, especially the *Passion According to St. Matthew*. One night, while I was dressing to go out to dinner, she came to watch me, she hates it when I go out but that night she was happy, she approved of my dress; she prefers classic clothes and this was a long gown of straw-coloured silk, long sleeves, a low waistline. Do you like it, Tigrela? I asked and she came and put her paws on my lap, licked my chin lightly so as not to spoil my make-up and began to pull on my amber necklace with her teeth. Do you want it? I asked and she growled, polite but firm. I took off the necklace and put it over her head. She saw her reflection in the mirror, her eyes moist with pleasure. Then she licked my hand and went off with the necklace dangling about her neck, the largest beads dragging on the floor. When she is calm, her eyes turn a pale yellow, the colour of amber.

Does Aninha sleep in the apartment? I asked and Romana gave a start, as if she had just then become conscious of the fact that Aninha arrived early and left at nightfall, the two of them slept there alone. I gave her a long look and she laughed. I know, you think I'm crazy but nobody understands it from the outside, it's complicated. And yet so simple, you have to get inside to understand. I put on my jacket, it had gotten cooler. Do you remember, Romana? Our graduation party, I still have the picture, you bought some shoes for the dance that were too tight, you ended up dancing barefoot during the waltz. I saw you whirling around from far away, your hair loose, your dress light. I thought it was beautiful, you dancing barefoot like that. She looked at me attentively but didn't hear a single word I said. We're vegetarians, I've always been a vegetarian, you know. I didn't know. Tigrela eats only legumes, fresh herbs and milk with honey, meat doesn't come in through our door because meat gives you bad breath. And ideas, she said, clutching my hand, I need you. I bent over to listen, but the waiter's arm reached out to empty the ash tray and she became frivolous again, interested in the cleanliness of the ash tray, had I by any chance tried milk, watercress and honey beaten up together? The recipe was very simple, you just whipped everything in the blender and then strained it through a sieve, she added, extending a hand, do you have the time, sir? Is there someone you have to meet, something you have to do? I inquired and she replied no, she had nothing coming up. Absolutely nothing, she repeated and I had the impression she grew paler as her mouth opened slightly to return to her obscure calculations. With the tip of her tongue she caught the diminished ice cube and chewed it. It hasn't happened yet but it's going to happen, she said with slight difficulty as the ice burned her tongue. I kept still. A large gulp of whisky seemed to give her back some warmth. One of these nights when I go home the porter may come running up to tell me, did madam know? From one of these terraces . . . but then, maybe he won't say anything and I'll have to take the elevator up, acting very natural so he doesn't notice anything, to gain one more day. Sometimes we meditate and I don't know what the results might be. I taught her so many things. I learned so many others, she said, beginning a gesture but not finishing it. Had she told me Aninha was the one who trimmed her finger-nails? She would offer her a paw without the least resistance, but she didn't let her brush her teeth, she had very sensitive gums. I brought her a natural-bristle toothbrush, you have to brush in a downward direction, very lightly, mint-flavoured toothpaste. She didn't use dental floss because she never ate anything fibrous, but if she ever needed it, she knew where to find the dental floss.

I ordered a sandwich, Romana ordered raw carrots, well scrubbed. With salt, she advised, pointing to her empty glass.

We didn't speak while the waiter poured the whisky. When he left I started laughing, but is it really true, Romana? All this. She didn't answer, she was adding up her memories again, and one of them was leaving her short of air: she breathed deeply, loosening the knot in her scarf. Then I saw the purple bruise on her neck; I looked toward the wall. I could see in the mirror when she re-tied the knot and sniffed her whisky. She smiled. Tigrela knew when whisky wasn't genuine, to this day I can't distinguish them but one night she gave a paw-swat to a bottle and it flew across the room, why did you do that, Tigrela? She didn't answer. I went to look at the pieces of the bottle and saw that it was a brand that had once given me a hallucinating hangover. Can you believe she knows more about my life than Yasbeck? And Yasbeck was more jealous of me than anyone else, he kept a detective watching me. She pretends not to pay any attention but her pupils dilate and spill over, like black ink spreading over her eyes, have I mentioned those eyes? In them I see her emotions, her jealousy. She becomes intractable, she refuses her shawl, her pillow and goes into the garden which I had specially planted, a miniature jungle. She stays there all day long and through the night, hidden in a thicket in the foliage. I can call her until I drop but she won't come, her nose moist with dew or tears.

I stared at the ring of water left on the tabletop by the glass. But Romana, wouldn't it be more humane to send her to the zoo? Let her go back to being an animal, I think it's cruel to impose your own cage on her this way, what if she's happier in the other kind? You've enslaved her. And ended up enslaving yourself, you must have. Aren't you at least going to give her freedom to choose? Impatiently, Romana dipped her carrot into the salt. She licked it. Freedom is comfort, my dear, which Tigrela knows also. She has every comfort, just as Yasbeck had before disposing of me.

And now you want to dispose of her, I said. At one of the tables a man started to sing a snatch of opera at the top of his lungs, but quickly his voice was submerged in laughter. Romana spoke so quickly I had to interrupt, slower, I can't understand you. She reined in her onrush of words, but soon they began galloping ahead again, as if she hadn't much time left. Our most violent fight was because of him, Yasbeck, you know, all the confusion of an old love who suddenly reappears, sometimes he calls and then we sleep together, she knows perfectly well what's happening, once she heard us talking, when I got back she was awake, waiting for me as still as a statue in front of the door, of course I covered up as well as I could, but she's intelligent, she sniffed at me until she discovered the scent of a man on me, she went wild. I think now I'd like to have a unicorn, you know, one of those blondish horses with a pink horn on its forehead, I saw one in a tapestry, it was so in love with the princess she offered it a mirror to look at itself, waiter, please can you tell me the time? And bring more ice! She went for two days without eating, tigerish, continued Romana. She spoke slowly now, her voice thick, one word after the other with calculated little adjustments in the empty spaces. Two days without eating, dragging her necklace and her arrogance around the house. I wondered, Yasbeck had promised to call and he didn't, he sent me a note, why is your phone dead? When I went to look I discovered the cord chewed completely through, the toothmarks all the way up and down the plastic. She didn't say a thing but I could feel her watching me through those slits of eyes, they can penetrate walls. I think that on that same day she read my thoughts, we began to distrust each other, but even so, do you see? she used to be so full of fervour. . . .

Used to be? I asked. She opened her hands on the table and challenged me, Why are you looking at me that way? What else could I do? She must have wakened around eleven, it's the time she always wakes up, she enjoys the night. Instead of milk, I filled her saucer with whisky and turned off the lights, when she's desperate she sees better in the dark and today she was desperate, because she overheard my conversation, she thinks I'm with him now. The door to the terrace is open, but then it's stayed open on other nights and nothing happened. But you never know, she's so unpredictable, she added in a whisper. She wiped the salt from her fingers on a paper napkin. I'll be on my way. I'll go back to the apartment trembling because I never know whether or not the porter's coming to tell me that a young lady has thrown herself off one of the terraces, naked except for an amber necklace.

Translated by Eloah F. Giacomelli

The Usurper

BEATRIZ GUIDO

AT THE AGE OF eight, Beatriz Guido decided that she wanted to go to a convent school "because nuns are so mysterious." Her education and her upbringing (her family belonged to the Argentine upper middle class) became the subject matter of her stories and novels: closed worlds with dark sexual undercurrents, social rituals, and rites of passage. Her first novel, La casa del ángel (The House of the Stone Angel) contains all these elements; it follows the awakening of a rich young girl, raped by one of her father's friends the evening before a duel. Like most of her work, it was made into a film by her husband, the director Leopoldo Torres Nilsson. Beatriz Guido is now the Argentine cultural attaché in Spain.

ON SUNDAYS MY father would saddle the white horse with its finest livery and silver trimmings, lift her out of her wheel-chair and, holding her against his breast, would cross the town of Mercedes all the way up to the Cathedral. Mother and I would follow behind, in a low carriage so as not to disturb (it occurs to me now) the view of her towering hair-do which the maids would brush for hours to make her look taller. I am still haunted by her perfume of cheap lacquer which protected her hair against the wind—the breeze rather —which the summer days sometimes allowed us.

The tobacco fields lay only a few miles away from our house: I say "our" house because we slept there, even though sometimes we spent the night on the top floor of the general stores my father owned throughout the northeast of the prov-ince. Once we had reached the Cathedral, the beggars and a few of my father's clerks would run and help my sister Victo-ria dismount, and then carry her on a sort of throne made out of velvet up to the very first row inside the church. I think that in the vestry was a special orthopaedic chair for her, and on grand occasions they would sit her in it with a satin pouch on her lap, and wheel her through the main courtyard to make the collection. Everyone gave willingly.

"An angel!" they would say. "She's like an angel!" "Every day more beautiful." "A saint." "The other is not at all like her . . . and yet so like her."

They were right. My twin sister Victoria and myself looked so alike that the farm-hands thought of us as a kind of mira-cle. Little did they know that our likeness even went as far as demolishing that most revolutionary of all Argentine discov-eries: our fingerprints were identical. Especially the right thumb; the left thumb perhaps not, but only a strong magni-fying glass could have spotted a shadow along the middle line (as my father used to say when he had to go and fetch me back from Bella Vista, where I used to escape during the harvest with whatever farm-hands brought blood to my cheeks). But spiritually we *were* not alike. I think that even during our first year of life we were different. My mother would tell us how I used to dig my teeth into her breasts, and how I used to tear apart any toy or rattle I was given. Even the overripe pomegranate or the avocado stone were prey to my voracity.

But then the accident happened, the accident that left my sister paralyzed for life: before our very eyes Father drove a stake through the pony that had thrown her among the creepers and the tobacco leaves, and left it to die devoured by the vultures. Nobody could explain the unquestionable fatality of the fall. From that moment Victoria—whose laughter, whose tenderness never vanished, and whose tears were like a silent offering—was the happiest of mortals, and the only object of Father's adoration. He never tried to hide from me the fact that the town felt obliged to elect Victoria Queen of the Floral Games: the prize was a trip to Buenos Aires for the coronation of the provincial poet laureate, whose head she would crown with tobacco leaves.

When my father used to come back drunk from Empedrado or Goya, at three in the morning, Victoria would meet him with fruit curd and warm milk, and he would kiss her hands and feet, while my mother slept sitting upright for fear of ruffling her lacquered hair-do. Sometimes, at Easter, on my parents' anniversary, Mother would dress Victoria in her wedding-gown; not to be unfair, she would dress me up as the groom, and we would act out a mock-ceremony in which Victoria would be Mother and I Father in a Charles Chaplin jacket and a starched shirt with pearl and diamond buttons. Perhaps it was the only time in the year when I saw my mother laugh without being afraid of leaving a trace of wrinkles on her translucent china-doll's skin.

We lived constantly surprised by our physical likeness, a likeness I never managed to hide in spite of beauty creams, powders and lipstick. Many times we played the game of the mirror: we would place an empty Venetian frame in the living-room, and, dressed in the same way—my sister sitting in a velvet colonial armchair and I in its twin—we would imitate each other's gestures for hours, while my parents' guests stared at us in amazement and Eulalia, my mother's only friend, would say: "Marina, don't spend so much time looking at yourself in the mirror!"

We used to sleep in the same room; we were afraid of the empty farm-house, always under the menacing eye of strangers from the provinces, men driven crazy by wine, *grapa* and cheap gin, strong like the sun in the desert.

Our house was a target for their violence: burning torches, bottles, balls of mud were thrown against our walls. They were answered by a bullet between the eyes shot by the man in charge of guarding our sleep, from up upon the marble balustrade of the still-standing tower.

How many times Victoria and I would see the body being picked up and then, on the next day, somewhere in the bush, the dug-up pile of dirt would appear. But we both kept silent because we knew that underneath lay the body of a worker who had lost his mind after drinking the cheap liquor sold in our general stores. I wasn't afraid of them.

After the age of fourteen, when one of my father's brothers took my virginity under the grand piano in the living-room (after which we went on sipping our tea and nibbling at sweetmeats dipped in aniseed) and I guessed somehow that when our body split inside my mother's womb I had become incapable of bearing children—after that I realized that, if I was not to die of boredom, I needed to satisfy myself like a man, just as men do, with the same need to know them in their cries, their yelps, in the indiscriminate shape of their bodies. I never could overcome the disgust I felt at the smell of alcohol in all of them, but mint tablets and imported myrurgia extracts (sold in our stores) helped me bear the entertainment undauntedly, the need for which led me, beneath the scorching sun, during the long siestas, down to the river to meet someone who had barely glanced at me, or helped me get off my horse, or a wandering circus performer, a tightrope-walker, whose ephemeral passage through the town made him invulnerable to gossip.

I remember a Hungarian acrobat who would lock the door of his room in the small hotel, while I excited myself watching his twists and loops, watching his silent Filipino assistant polish the "ropes of death"—his trained serpents. Without saying a single word, I would writhe among the antique lace sheets of the Fratellini hotel on a hot February afternoon, and the fans on the ceiling would cool my soaking hair and his old muscles which tempted death.

Without saying a word, I felt I could disappear in a spell of passion and ecstasy, a spell always within reach. It didn't trouble me in the least to hold the eyes of a worker or a foreman on mass Sundays, or during the huge barbecues with which my father celebrated his impiety and his fortune.

I would run away with an occasional beau to the stables or the tower, and taunt his ignorance with terrible stories that afterwards would spread through the town. Didn't they know that the bull's eye we used for shooting was an Indian caught by my grandfather, an Indian who had become both target and trophy? The lost souls of the dead Indians wandered through the passageways of the house, and their groans could be heard coming from the cupboards; during storms, the town witches would read out their curses against us.

I could see how my beaux frightened Victoria, when, during the siestas that followed the long lunches, I would lead my fortunate and wary friends "to rest"—as I would both modestly and insolently put it. They would escape trying to hide their fear, because they said they could hear those groans coming from a trapdoor in the stables or from the cellars, the groans of the dead souls of the ignorant Mataco Indians. And while my frenzy would feed on their terror and my contempt, I would think up a story to startle Victoria.

"Would you like to have barbecued Indian ribs for dinner tonight?" I would ask.

"There are no Indians," Victoria would say. "Only half-breeds."

"I mean the ghosts of Indians, you idiot! As if this were the Day of Judgement and each one of them found their own body, and Grandad were to shoot them all over again, just because his dear Vicky is so fond of their meat!"

Victoria would pass a finger over her lips and bless me on the forehead and say:

"You musn't voice wicked thoughts; let them drain away through the blood."

"Down the sewers you mean," I, Marina, would say.

Victoria, her head on my lap, would insist:

"The holy angels take our wicked thoughts away from us."

Victoria and I attended the same lessons with teachers brought over from Goya in my father's landrover.

We also travelled to Buenos Aires and Switzerland, in search of a cure that would make Victoria walk, even though I believe she never really cared. A world of servants drifted around her. The bathtub was a pool made out of Carrara marble and mirrors which reflected my body next to hers, a body that had lost none of its charm. The servants would celebrate her immersion crying *Alleluyah*, and afterwards piously dry her forehead. Victoria would gently ask for fresh grapes, peaches and plums—the bath lasted two or three hours in the hope of an impossible recovery.

Vicky—as we would sometimes call her—would ask to be wheeled through the slums in her chair, carrying with her the pious consolation of her charity to the poor who saw in her the Holy Virgin of Itatí seated in a luxurious throne on wheels. She would never complain—never a curse or an unworthy prophecy. Well, only once: that one time when she thought that no one, not even I, was looking.

Victoria had wheeled her chair through the passageways. She thought she heard a faraway moan, the wailing of Indians growing louder as her chair drew near it. She never guessed that I had caught a cat in a skunk-trap. She approached the window from where she thought the pitiful crying came and then, suddenly, shattered the glass in a fit of violence. Outside a furious storm had broken over the house, and the wind and rain began to blow into the room. I crept into her bed and held her in my arms.

"If you went into politics you'd be governor in no time," I said to her one day, and she answered, while brushing my hair:

"It would be the only case in history of two governors. . . . Because, of course, we'd govern together."

Suddenly she said: "Where do you go at night? I'm so afraid of what might happen to you. . . . That's the only thing I regret: not being able to come along with you."

"At night I enjoy myself," I answered. "Otherwise I'd have to leave 'La Alborada,' this house I hate from the very depth of my soul."

The farm-hand who drove our jeep got off quickly and helped set up Victoria's wheelchair. In the middle of the field was a small clump of trees next to a river, and further away, a mound of earth some thirty or forty metres large.

"Look there," I said to Victoria. "There lie the bodies of the dead Matacos. The grass has grown over them and the earth is dry, but they are there. Come and see." We drew near until we almost touched the heap. "There must be some one hundred, two hundred bodies here. Children, young men, old men. Anyone who stood in our way ended up here, and they are the ones whose spirits now haunt us, drunk, at night. Even if no one in town talks about it any more, everyone remembers."

Victoria and I waited for a moment in silence, wrapped in the wind that was blowing from the river.

Perhaps it was then that my curiosity was aroused. What was Vicky's life like beneath the sheets that covered her naked body, after the servants had smeared her skin with oil. . . ?

Her only male friend was Pablo Fuentes, who lived at the entrance to the town of Mercedes with his mother, and whose father was killed in a fight at one of the barracks. Pablo grew up with us, kind and wise, and every day would travel to Corrientes to finish his studies in Medicine. While he studied he made his living giving injections at the Santa Lucia drugstore, and driving an ambulance—the only one in town—which my father had donated. As there was no one else to drive it, it became Pablo's property—Pablo who in our minds was barely an adolescent.

Pablo's only pleasure was to sound the siren, just as if we lived in a big city, as soon as he arrived at the gates of the farm, so that we'd immediately know of his presence. Victoria's face would light up and she would have me wheel her out to meet him. We would both get into the ambulance and play the same game over and over again. I was the one who would pretend to have had an accident.

"I'm dying! I was struck in the heart!" And I would force

Pablo to give me a check-up. He, shyly, would open up my blouse, put a mask on me pretending I needed oxygen, and then we'd race across the fields, sounding the siren as if we were some kind of a whining runaway horse.

Pablo was tall, strong, slightly cross-eyed. As a child he had been a choirboy in church, until one Palm Sunday I and my cousins from Resistencia put a firecracker inside his robes. He told us he could not stand the fun made of him as he carried the banner in the processions, and that he only helped at mass for a dish of *feixoada* or rice, or some tobacco.

It was my mother who suggested that he might make a splendid driver to carry Victoria and her wheelchair.

Vicky and Pablo shared a world of their own. His was a dedicated job that grew with time, and he had a good Samaritan air about him that made me sick. There was not a fire for which he would not put on a fireman's helmet to help evacuate the people, while the temperature rose to over forty degrees in the shade.

I, perhaps to provoke them, would let the house dogs die of thirst, or a she-cat who had just given birth. I imagined that their wailing at night would justify the cruel stories that spread through the town.

Pablo became one of us, and my father, to reward him, gave him one of the shacks at the entrance of the farm. When Pablo's mother died, he became even more attached to us, somewhat morose, only smiling when wheeling Victoria's chair around, through the courtyards and the gardens, inside the bush, having picnics in the tobacco fields, coming back home long after dark.

I had not tried to be deliberately cruel, but I said:

"What *do* you do with Pablo? You're not going to tell me he hasn't even kissed you." I saw at once that I had opened secret doors, and her eyes begged for either my pity or my silence.

I decided to spy on them.

One afternoon, after many days of rain, coming back from Corrientes, I stopped at Pablo's place. Through the blinds I saw, I learnt, I understood how kings make love. My sister—myself—was sitting upon a platform covered with a red satin curtain, like the ones that hung at home. Vicky was no longer in her wheelchair: Pablo had placed her high upon an imperial throne. Then he started kissing her all over her body, for well over an hour, while she caressed his naked skin. With the craft of a surgeon he combed her hair apart, opened her lips, drew with his fingers her features, while music by Vivaldi leaked from a cranky phonograph. They made love like the ritual of Consecrating the Host, a ritual conducted by a saint.

The ritual, the possession drew well into the night; to punish myself, I stayed on for the aftermath, while my knees felt too weak to hold me. I felt my face flushed and I saw myself in the living-room mirror, unable to imitate the movements of that love.

Perhaps after that day I felt impotent and broken, and as lonely in the world as the land which had bred in me both violence and boredom. I never was the same again.

Victoria became my enemy. I could not hide my anger, and my long absences were even more frequent than before. I tried to show my father, in front of Victoria, my promiscuity, but he barely said anything, obsessed with his own life and his ambition. My mother worried in silence.

It was Ash Wednesday: Carnival, with masks and costumes. I asked Victoria to come with me to a party in the second barrack. The workers were preparing to go back to their province and Vicky was supposed to make an appearance among them: my father had managed to have her chosen Beauty Queen of Corrientes. Under the light of the moon I wheeled her in, both of us dressed in lace and gauze, to witness the last rites of Carnival.

The Carnival parade, the shabby and improvised Carnival put together by the workers as an excuse to get drunk, came forth to meet us. Puppet-heads made out of cane, men dressed up in oilcloths and potato-sacks, painted faces—all looked like penitents on a Holy Week procession. Some covered their heads with white elastic socks, delirious ghosts in makeshift costumes, using the kettles in which they boiled the tobacco leaves as infernal drums.

I had begun to drink early in the day, and now carried a bottle of brandy hanging from Victoria's chair. I didn't force her to drink: she asked me, as if she needed strength to face the workers. We got there quite late at night when all the workers were already drunk: I chose my partner and left Victoria among the other men.

I realized that there were some women there, and children: they were just as drunk as the men. Among the tobacco sheaves I undressed several times: several times, because I would get dressed again to go back into the barrack, but desire and the need for time to complete its circle drew me back.

When all was silent, I whipped the face of the last man who had taken me and left him sleeping among the tobacco leaves.

I entered the barrack.

I had a hard time finding her, because they had abandoned her in a heap on the floor, under the masks and cane puppets. There she lay, next to her wheelchair, dead and raped several times. My sister Victoria. I never hesitated, not for a moment. I hid her clothes; I painted her dead eyes and her dead lips; I sat in her chair and I began to whine and moan until they discovered us next morning: the farm-hands, my father —who never stopped kissing me—and Pablo Fuentes, who now wheels my chair around, wipes my tears, accompanies me to the cemetery and drives me around in his ambulance. I, Victoria, have discovered that a body can, sometimes, belong to another body.

Translated by Alberto Manguel

How the Monkey Lost the Fruit of His Labor

LYDIA CABRERA

LYDIA CABRERA IS Cuba's most famous woman writer, respected both by intellectuals still living in Cuba and by those in exile. She was born in Havana in 1900 and, after studying in Paris, returned to Cuba to explore its wealth of Afro-Cuban traditions. She now lives in Miami. Her own fiction consists of retellings of many of these fables and legends in a style as simple as possible, in an effort to preserve their oral quality. In a conversation with Suzanne Jill Levine, Lydia Cabrera explained why she believes that, while in the United States no African traditions survive, African culture is still alive in Spanish Cuba and Portuguese Brazil. "First, there was the relative absence of racial prejudice among the Spaniards, and second, the slave laws among the Portuguese and the Spaniards were less intolerant than the laws established by the North Americans. For example, in the United States the blacks were denied the right to have meetings, and their drums and musical instruments were taken away. In Cuba, the blacks had their cabildos, *which were like clubs. . . . Each tribe had its* cabildo, *where they would dance and play their music and, under the auspices of their Catholic owners, perform their rituals. History has not been very fair to the Spanish, after all."*

JUAN GANGA TOLD his wife, "I think I'll clear an acre and plant some rice."

"Go ahead, do whatever you want," answered Viviana Angola.

Juan Ganga almost never finished what he started. His enthusiasm invariably waned by noontime.

But this time Juan Ganga was determined to harvest rice.

He spent a day levelling the field. He cut down a tree or two. The next morning, finding the entire field cleared, he gathered sticks until vespers. The following day, he found all the deadwood burned. He returned at daybreak with a hoe and hoed leisurely until sunset. When he returned the next dawn, the land was completely hoed.

Ah! The rice had ripened and Juan Ganga happily decided that the moment had arrived to show off his work to Viviana Angola before beginning the harvest. But then a monkey arrived and told him, "Juan Ganga, the rice is ready for reaping. When are you going to begin?"

"I thought I'd start tomorrow."

"Very well, but you won't be alone. We have both worked on this field and I, too, have every right to profit from my work. Isn't that fair?"

"Yes, sir."

"You come tomorrow with your helpers and I'll come with mine. I'll have a hundred monkeys with me. You begin with your folk at one end of the field and I'll start harvesting on the other side with the monkeys until we meet in the middle somewhere. And whoever gathers more, well . . . isn't that fair?"

That afternoon, Juan Ganga returned home discouraged, gloomy. He didn't dare—it pained him—to tell Viviana Angola what had happened, for each time she had heard him boast of how swiftly he had levelled, cleared, hoed, and planted his acre, she had done nothing more than say "Hum!" To have to confess to her . . . still, Viviana Angola could fix anything. What a woman! Whenever her name was mentioned, people always said, "That woman is worth her weight in gold," or, "She's priceless." Basking in the envy of others, Juan Ganga himself proudly affirmed, "My woman is worth as much as any man." There was one and only one Viviana Ganga in the land. . . . Certainly Viviana scolded him and even punished him, hurling at him the first hard object she could grasp. But it's also true that whenever Viviana got angry, she was always in the right, and her outbursts were only fleeting. Her rages, no matter how justified, never lasted more than a few seconds. Once the dangerous moment of the explosion passed, all her anger vanished. Her happy disposition and jesting nature, coupled with her heart of gold, made her forgive very quickly. Yes, Viviana forgave all, everything. She had as great a capacity for pardon as for work and happiness!

Juan Ganga would have given anything to take her to his field and show her his ripe rice to prove that he hadn't lied, that he had worked. Covering himself with glory in her eyes, he could have told her, "There! You see?"

Now, she didn't know how to explain it, but when Viviana Angola saw him so discouraged and pensive, with such dejected eyes fixed on the ground, she suspected something serious: "Juan Ganga, you tell me what's wrong this very minute."

And Juan Ganga told her everything.

"I'm sunk! Lost! One hundred good men couldn't finish in days what those monkeys could do in only a few hours."

"We'll figure a way out of this scrape," said Viviana Angola. And since she couldn't go long without laughing for one reason or another—no one in this world ever laughed with such pleasure nor had a more contagious laugh—Viviana greeted Juan Ganga's predicament gleefully.

"You don't understand, Viviana. Those monkeys are unstoppable. They pick ten plants where they've only sown five!"

Finally, Viviana Angola, who never walked but ran, hurried away to buy a bunch of jingle bells.

"Jingle bells?"

"Leave it to me. I know what I'm doing."

Then she went to look for the men needed to help harvest the rice. Fifty would be enough if they all worked together; she rounded them up.

Viviana Angola showed up at the rice field at God's sunrise, followed by Juan Ganga and his assistants. The monkeys were already waiting there. They stood in the middle of the field, between the two sections.

The men took one side; the monkeys, the other; Viviana Angola stood in the center. The Chief Monkey gave the signal: "Begin!"

The two groups advance across the field. The men aren't exactly falling asleep, but Juan Ganga is right. As hard as they try, they can't keep up with the monkeys. While the men bundle one sheaf, the monkeys do six.

Juan Ganga crosses his arms.

"We're sunk!"

But Viviana Angola doesn't lose heart. Smiling and vivacious, she begins to gently sway, swinging her shoulders and back as she chants:

> *Ayelelé tá kundé*
> *Kuna makando munango*
> *endile!*

Soon there is a rich, enchanting melody that stirs the curiosity of the industrious monkeys.

"Listen," they tell one another, interrupting their work and straining their ears.

Viviana Angola sings. . . .

She turns toward the men and gently lifts the hem of her skirt. Then she turns toward the monkeys and raises her skirt to her waist. Oh!

"Look!" the monkeys shriek, overjoyed.

"Look! Just look!"

Viviana Angola shakes her hips suddenly:

Goringóro-góro-góro-góro . . .

"And do you hear *that?* She rings!" they say, more amazed each time.

"Did you see? . . ."

"Yes. . . ."

"Yes, and now I just saw . . ."

"Oh!"

"Wait!—look again!"

"Now—look! Now! Now! Listen! And do you *see?*"

Viviana Angola turns toward the part of the field where the men work unceasingly. She shows her ankle. . . .

The monkeys and their Chief stand rooted, absorbed . . . staring.

Then Viviana Angola turns toward them; one moment she shows them—a second, no more—just what keeps ringing and sparkling.

Goringóro-góro-góro-góro

Their frenzied curiosity mounting, the monkeys dart about frantically, jumping from side to side but not harvesting rice. No. To get a better look at just what Viviana Angola is concealing, they throw themselves stupidly to the ground, straining to see even more.

Some shriek stupidly, others jubilantly, impatiently. . . .

If Viviana Angola would only stay still a moment with her skirt raised! What does Má Viviana have that chimes and shines so?

The monkeys' sheaves have all fallen to the ground; the men snatch them up.

Ayelé tá kundé
Kuna Makando
endile!

"Look!"
"Now! . . . Now!"

Goringóro-góro-góro-góro

"Oh!"

The Chief, stupidly, also stands there, rooted in place, waiting for Viviana Angola to raise her skirt just once more to satisfy their curiosity. The men keep right on working steadily.

Goringóro-góro-góro-góro

And the monkeys ended up without rice . . . and without ever knowing what was hidden, what was so fascinating, what tinkled and twinkled under the skirts of Viviana Angola.

Translated by Mary Caldwell and Suzanne Jill Levine

Death of the Tiger

ROSARIO CASTELLANOS

MAGIC REALISM AND *political realism, the two main currents
in the literature of Latin American countries, appear in the
very first pages ever written in Spanish in the New World. On
the one hand, early magic realism is found in the fanciful
descriptions of the land as the conquistadores saw it, their
minds fed on medieval imagery. On the other, political realism, the factual description of the colonial regime and the
fate of the exploited Indians, makes its appearance in 1552,
in the Very Brief Description of the Destruction of the Indies by Father Bartolomé de Las Casas, a Dominican priest
who had taught the Catholic faith in America. Both themes
surface in the work of Rosario Castellanos, who began her literary career as a poet, publishing between 1948 and 1960 a
series of intimate lyrics that explore "the geography of
women." The combination of social and fantastic literature is
clearer in her best novel,* Oficio de tinieblas (Labours of
Darkness), *published in 1962, and in her collection of stories,*
Ciudad Real—*the chronicle of Indian life in contemporary
Mexico—from which the following story was taken.*

THE BOLOMETIC TRIBE consisted of families of the same blood. Their protecting spirit, their *waigel*, was the tiger, whose name they were entitled to bear because of their courage and their daring.

After immemorial pilgrimages (fleeing from the coast, from the sea and its suicidal temptation), the men of this race finally established themselves in the mountainous region of Chiapas, in a plateau rich in pastures, woods and water. There prosperity made them lift their heads up high, and filled their hearts with haughtiness and greed. Frequently the Bolometic would come down from the mountains to feed on the possessions of the neighbouring tribes.

With the arrival of the white men, known as *caxlanes*, the belligerent and fiery Bolometic leapt into battle with such force that they dashed themselves against the invading iron and crumbled to pieces. Worse than vanquished, aghast, the Bolometic felt for the first time in their own flesh the rigours of defeat. They were stripped of their belongings, thrown into jail, forced into slavery. Those who managed to escape (their newly acquired poverty inspired them, made them invisible to their enemies' fury) sought refuge at the foot of the hills. There they stopped to look back and see what the calamity had left them, and there they began a precarious life in which the memory of past greatness slowly vanished, and history became a dying fire that no one was capable of rekindling.

From time to time, a few of the bravest men would climb down to the neighbouring settlements and trade in their harvest; they would also visit the sanctuaries, praying to the Higher Powers that They cease tormenting their *waigel*, their tiger, whom the shaman could hear, roaring and wounded, high above in the thicket. The Bolometic were generous in their offerings, and yet their prayers were not answered. Their tiger was yet to receive many more wounds.

The *caxlanes'* greed cannot be stifled either by force or with gifts. It sleeps not. It watches, wide awake, within the white men, within their children, within their children's children. And the *caxlanes* march on, never sleeping, trampling the earth with the iron hoofs of their horses, casting around their hawk's eyes, nervously clicking their whips.

The Bolometic saw the advancing threat but did not run, as before, to lift the weapons they no longer had the courage to wield. They drew together, trembling with fear, to discuss their own conduct, as if they were about to appear before a demanding and merciless tribunal. They would not defend themselves: how could they? They had forgotten the art of war and had not learnt that of arguing. They would humble themselves. But the white man's heart is made of stuff that does not grow soft with prayers. And mercy is a fine plum on a captain's helmet, but does not dust the sand that dries the clerk's legal documents.

"In this speaking paper all truth is set. And the truth is that all this land, with its hillsides good for the sowing of corn, with its pine forests to be felled for logs and fire-wood, with its rivers good for mills, is the property of Don Diego Mijangos y Orantes, who has proven direct lineage from that other Don Diego Mijangos, conquistador, and from the later Mijangos, respectable slave traders. Therefore you, Sebastian Gomez Escopeta, and you, Lorenzo Perez Diezmo, and you, Juan Dominguez Ventana, or whatever your name is, you're not wanted here, you're taking up room that doesn't belong to you, and that is a crime punished by the law. Off with you, you good-for-nothings. Away."

Centuries of submission had deformed that race. Quickly they lowered their faces in obeisance; meekly they turned their backs to run. The women went ahead, carrying the children and a few necessary utensils. The elderly men followed on slow feet. And further back, protecting the exodus, the men.

Hard days, with no goal in sight. Leaving one place because

it was unfriendly, and another not to fight over it with its owners. Provisions and vittles were scarce. Those whom hunger bit more cruelly than others dared to sneak out at night, near the maize fields, and under cover of darkness would steal a few ripe stalks of grain, a few edible leaves. But the dogs would sniff out the strangers and bark their warning. The guards would arrive whirling their machetes and making such a racket that the intruders would flee, panic-stricken. But they would carry on their quest, starving, in hiding, the long hair bedraggled and the clothes in shreds.

Misery ravaged the tribe, badly protected from the harsh weather. The cold breathed upon them its lethal breath and shrouded them in a whitish, thick fog. First the children, who died without understanding why, their little fists tightly clenched as if trying to cling onto the last wisp of heat. Then the old people, huddled next to the campfire ashes, without uttering a single moan. The women hid themselves to die, with a last display of modesty, as in the happy old days they had hidden themselves to give birth.

These were the ones who stayed behind, those who would never see their new homeland. They finally set up camp on a high terrace, so high that it cut in two the white man's cold breath, a land swept by hostile winds, poor, scorned even by the vilest weeds and creepers, the earth showing its barren entrails through the deep cracks. The brackish water lay far away.

A few stole pregnant ewes and herded them in secret. The women set up a loom, waiting for the first shearing. Others ploughed the land, the inflexible, avaricious land. The rest set off on long journeys to pray for divine benevolence in sanctuaries set aside for holy worship.

But times were grim and hunger was on the rampage, going from house to house, knocking at every door with its bony hand.

The men, after meeting in council, decided to leave. The

women forewent the last mouthful so as not to hand them an empty basket. And at the crossroads they said their farewells.

On and on. The Bolometic never rested, even at night. Their torches could be seen snaking down the blackness of the hills.

Now, in Ciudad Real men no longer live according to their whims or their needs. In the planning of this city of white men, of *caxlanes*, what ruled was the intelligence. The streets cross each other in geometrical patterns. The houses are of one and the same height, of one and the same style. A few display on their facades a coat of arms, because their owners are the descendants of those warriors—conquistadores, the first colonisers—whose deeds still ring with an heroic peal in certain family names: Marin, De la Tovilla, Mazariegos.

During the colonial centuries and the first decades of independence, Ciudad Real was the provincial seat of government. It boasted the opulence and abundance of commerce, it became the beacon of culture. But in the years to come, only one high function still kept its seat in Ciudad Real: the bishopric.

Now the city's splendour was a thing of the past. Decay gnawed at its very innards. Men with neither temerity nor vision, full of their own importance, deep in the contemplation of the past, gave up the political sceptre, let go the reins of commerce, closed the book of intellectual endeavours. Surrounded by a tight ring of Indian communities, all silently hostile, Ciudad Real always maintained with them a one-sided relationship. The systematic plunder was answered by a latent grumbling that a few times exploded into bloody uprisings. And each time Ciudad Real seemed less capable of stifling these by itself. Neighbouring towns—Comitan, Tuxtla, Chiapa de Corzo—came to its aid. Towards them flew the wealth, fame, command. Ciudad Real became nothing but a presumptuous and empty shell, a scarecrow that only scared the Indian soul, stubbornly attached to fear.

The Bolometic crossed the first streets amid the silent disapproval of the passersby who, with squeamish gestures, avoided brushing that offensive misery.

The Indians examined the spectacle before their eyes with curiosity, insistence, and lack of understanding. The massive walls of the *caxlanes'* temples weighed upon them almost as if they were obliged to carry that weight on their shoulders. The exquisite beauty of the ornaments—certain iron railings, the detailed carving of some of the stones—awoke in the Bolometic the desire to destroy them. They laughed at the sudden appearance of an object whose purpose they could not guess: fans, porcelain figures, lace clothing. They remained in ecstasy in front of a photographer's samples: postcards in which a melancholy lady appeared, meditating next to a broken column, while in the distant horizon sunk the also melancholy sun.

And people? How did the Bolometic see the people? They did not recognize the pettiness of these little men, short, plump, red-cheeked, the lees of a full-blooded, intrepid race. In front of their eyes they only saw the lightning which, in the past, had struck them down. And through the ugliness and decadence, the superstitious soul of the defeated could still make out the mysterious sign of the omnipotent *caxlan* god.

The women of Ciudad Real, the *coletas*, shuffled along the streets with small reticent steps, like doves; the eyes lowered, the cheeks blushing under the rough stroke of the wind. Silence and mourning went with them. And when they spoke, they spoke with that moss-like voice which puts tiny children to sleep, comforts the sick, helps the dying. The voice of those who watch the men go by from behind a windowpane.

The marketplace attracted the foreigners with its bustle. Here was the throne of plenty. Here was corn which stuffed the granaries with its yellow gold; here were red-blooded beasts, slaughtered, hanging from enormous hooks. The mellow fruits, delicious: peaches with their skins of eternal youth; bananas, strong and sturdy; the apple that, at times, tastes like the blade of a knife. And coffee, fragrant from a distance. And sweet preserves, baroque, christened with faraway tribal names: *tartaritas*, *africanas*. And bread with which God greets man every morning.

This was what the Bolometic saw, and they saw it with an amazement that was not touched with greed, that destroyed any thoughts of greed. With religious amazement.

The policeman in charge of watching over the marketplace was strolling aimlessly among the stalls, humming a song, waving away, here and there, a stray fly. But when he noticed the presence of the bunch of ragged loafers—he was accustomed to seeing them on their own, not in a group and with a leader—he automatically became suspicious. He gripped tight onto his stick, ready to swing it at the first attempt to steal, or to break that long and nebulous article of the law which he had never read but in whose existence he believed: causing public disturbances. But the Bolometic's intentions seemed to be peaceful. They had left the marketplace and were now looking for an empty spot among the pews of the Church of La Merced. On their haunches, the Indians patiently began to pick off their fleas and eat them. The policeman watched them from afar, pleased because contempt was on his side.

A gentleman who kept hovering around the Bolometic decided at last that he would speak to them. Fat, bald, full of forced merriment, he said to them in their own tongue:

"So, you there. Are you looking for work?"

The Bolometic looked at each other quickly and in panic. Each one left upon the other the responsibility of answering. Finally, the one who looked the most venerable—he was the most respected of the group because of his age and because he had once before been to Ciudad Real—asked:

"Can you find us work? Are you a 'collector'?"

"Exactly, my good fellow. And known to be fair and honest. My name is Juvencio Ortiz."

"Ah yes. Don Juvencio."

The comment was less an echo of his fame than a sign of good manners. Silence spread upon them like a stain. Don Juvencio drummed his fingers on the curve of his stomach, at the height of the waistcoat button where the watch chain should have hung. Remembering that he did not yet own a watch chain made him dig his spurs into the conversation.

"Well, then? Do we have a deal?"

But the Indians were in no hurry. There is never any hurry to fall into a trap.

"We came down from our lands. There's not much there, sir. The crops won't give."

"Exactly my point. Let's go to the office and sort out the details."

Don Juvencio began to walk, certain that the Indians would follow. Hypnotized by his assurance, the Indians went after him.

What Don Juvencio so pompously called his "office" was a dirty circular room on one of the streets off the marketplace. The furniture consisted of two wooden tables—more than once the splinters of their badly smoothed top had torn the sleeves of the only suits Don Juvencio and his associate possessed—a shelf full of papers, and two chairs of unsteady legs. On one of them, perched with the provisional attitude of a bird, was Don Juvencio's associate: a large profile, protected by a green plastic visor. He croaked as the visitors appeared before him.

"What good things are you bringing us, Don Juvencio?"

"Whatever I could get hold of, my dear friend. Competition is tough. 'Collectors' with fewer merits than mine—and I have a lawyer's degree, given by the Law School of Ciudad

Real—and less experienced than myself, steal our clients away."

"They use other methods. You've never made use of drink, for instance. A drunk Indian never notices what he does or what he agrees to do. But skimping on drink . . ."

"Not at all. But taking advantage of these poor souls when they are unconscious is, as His Illustrious Don Manuel Oropeza would say, a despicable thing to do."

Don Juvencio's associate showed his teeth in a wicked little smile.

"Well, your morals make our fortune. You were the one who said that everything might be lacking in this world, but there would always be Indians to spare. So we'll see. The farms that have put us in charge of their management run the risk of losing their crops for want of workers."

"Wise men change opinions, my dear partner. I also used to say. . . . But anyway, no need to complain. Here they are."

Don Juvencio made a wide gesture with his arm, like a magician unveiling his bag of tricks. But his associate's admiration remained undaunted.

"These?"

Don Juvencio saw himself obliged to change his tone of voice.

"These! Don't use that tone of voice with me. . . . What's wrong with them?"

Don Juvencio's associate shrugged his shoulders.

"They've got vultures pecking at their back, that's what's wrong. They'll never endure the climate on the coast. And you, who are so particular. . . ."

Don Juvencio drew close to his associate, lifting a finger in mock anger.

"You. . . . No wonder they call you a Jonah! Just remember, dear friend, the saying about minding one's own business. Is it our responsibility whether these Indians stand up or not to the climate? Our only obligation is to see that they arrive alive at the farm. What happens afterwards is none of our business."

And to avoid further discussion he moved towards the shelf and took out a pile of papers. After handing them over to his associate, Don Juvencio turned towards the Bolometic and ordered:

"Come on now, get in line. One by one, go up to this gentleman's desk and answer his questions. No lies, because the gentleman is a sorcerer and can hurt you badly. You know why he wears that visor? So as not to burn you with his eyes."

The Bolometic listened with ever-growing anguish. How would they be able to keep on hiding their true name?

They waited. But they knew it was useless.

And this is how the Bolometic placed the name of their *waigel*, the wounded tiger, under the will and command of those ink-stained hands.

"Pablo Gomez Bolom."

"Daniel Hernandez Bolom."

"Jose Dominguez Bolom."

Don Juvencio's associate drilled the Indians with useless suspicion. As usual, he thought, they were making fun of him. Afterwards, when they escaped from the farms without paying their debts, no one would be able to find them, because the place they said they came from did not exist, and the names they gave as theirs were false.

But no, in the name of the Holy Virgin of Caridad, enough! Don Juvencio's associate banged his fist on the table, furious. His knowledge of the Indian tongue was not enough to allow him to argue. Grumbling, all he said was:

"Bolom! I'll give you 'bolom'! Let's see the next one."

As soon as they had finished the associate let Don Juvencio know.

"Forty. What farm shall we send them to?"

"We'll service Don Federico Werner once and for all. He's the most urgent. Write down 'Coffee Plantation El Suspiro.' In Tapachuela."

As he wrote, his eyes protected by the green visor, Don Juvencio's associate insisted:

"Forty's not enough."

"Not enough? Forty Indians to pick the coffee beans on one farm? Worse is nothing. Not enough?"

"The forty won't reach the farm. They won't last the journey."

And Don Juvencio's associate turned the page, satisfied he was right.

With the advance money they had received, the Bolometic began their journey. Gradually, they left behind the wilderness of the hills and were shrouded in a sad, gritty breeze that broke into their misery. They could smell in the breeze sweet things. And they felt restless, like dogs on the trace of an unknown prey.

The height, leaving them so abruptly, shattered their eardrums. They were in pain, they bled from their ears. When the Bolometic reached the sea, they thought that its immense fury was mute.

The only presence that never left them was the cold, unwilling to abandon the bodies it had always held in its grip. Every day, at the same time, even when the tropical sun hit the grey stones, the cold would uncoil like a repulsive snake and slither over the Bolometic's bodies, stiffening their jaws, their arms and legs, with a terrible trembling. After that, the Bolometic would feel faint, shrunk, as if little by little the cold were shrivelling them in order to better fit in their awaiting tomb.

Those who survived that long journey were never able to

return. The debts would form a cage, link after link, chaining them to their new master. In the eardrum scars there echoed, more and more faintly, the voices of their women, calling them, and of their children, dying out.

The tiger in the hills was never heard of again.

Translated by Alberto Manguel

The Authors

Angel, Albalucía (Colombia, 1939–   ). Novelist, short-story writer, and folk-singer. Her first book, *Los girasoles en invierno*, won the "Esso" Prize in Bogota in 1966. She is the author of *Dos veces Alicia* (1972) and *Estaba la pájara pinta sentada en el verde limón* (1975).

Arredondo, Inés (Mexico, 1928–   ). Short-story writer, strongly influenced by the work of D. H. Lawrence. Her best stories were collected in *La señal* (1965).

Cabrera, Lydia (Cuba, 1900–   ). After studying in Paris, in 1927 Lydia Cabrera returned to her native Cuba to write about Afro-Cuban themes. In 1960 she moved to Miami, where she now lives. Her many books deal with Afro-Cuban subjects; a few are collections of stories: *Cuento negros de Cuba* (1936), *Ayapá* (1971).

Castellanos, Rosario (Mexico, 1925–1974). Poet, novelist, and short-story writer, Rosario Castellanos studied philosophy both in Mexico City and in Madrid. *Balun-Canan* (1957) is perhaps her most famous novel on the theme of the exploitation of the Indians.

Dávila, Amparo (Mexico, 1928–   ). Poet and short-story writer who obtained critical acclaim in the 1950s with three books of poems. Her collections of short stories—*Tiempo des-*

trozado (1959) and *Música concreta* (1964)—bring to Mexican fiction the fantastic elements of Kafka and Julio Cortázar.

Fagundes Telles, Lygia (Brazil, 1923–   ). Novelist and short-story writer, she published her first book, *O Cacto Vermelho*, a collection of tales, in 1944. Perhaps her best-known novel is *As Meninas*, winner of the 1973 Brazilian Academy of Letters Award. In 1969 her story "Antes do Baile Verde" won the International Women's Writing Prize at Cannes, and in 1972 she received the coveted Guimarâes Rosa Prize for her work. Several of her books, including *The Girl in the Photograph*, are available in English.

Garro, Elena (Mexico, 1920–   ). Playwright, novelist, and short-story writer. She achieved fame with her novel *Los recuerdos del porvenir* (1963), which was awarded the important Xavier Villarrutia Prize. Her several one-act plays were collected under the title *Un hogar sólido* (1958) and her stories in *La semana de colores* (1963). She married (and then divorced) the poet Octavio Paz.

Gorodischer, Angélica (Argentina, 1930–   ). Science-fiction writer. She has published several volumes of short stories—among them *Cuentos con soldados* (1965), *Las pelucas* (1968), *Casta luna electrónica* (1977), *Trafalgar* (1979)—and one novel, *Opus dos* (1967).

Guido, Beatriz (Argentina, 1925–   ). Novelist, short-story writer, and scriptwriter. Her first novel, *La casa del ángel* (1954), established her as one of the best-selling writers in Spanish. Among her later books are *La caída* (1956), *Fin de fiesta* (1958), and *El incendio y las vísperas* (1964). Most of her novels were made into films by her husband, Leopoldo Torres Nilsson.

Heker, Liliana (Argentina, 1943–   ). One of the most interesting short-story writers of her generation. Her first book,

Los que vieron la zarza (1966) established her reputation. She has since published *Acuario* (1972), *Las peras del mal* (1982), and one novel, *Un resplandor que se apagó en el mundo* (1977).

Kociancich, Vlady (Argentina, 1941–). Novelist and short-story writer. After studying for several years with Jorge Luis Borges, she began writing fiction. Her novel *La octava maravilla* (1981) was an immediate success. *Coraje* (1968) was her first book of short stories.

Lispector, Clarice (Brazil, 1922–). One of the most celebrated of modern Brazilian writers since the appearance of her book of short stories, *Laços de Familia* (1960). Among her best novels are *A Maça no Escuro* (1961) and *A Paixao Segundo G.H.* (1964). A few of her books and short stories have appeared in translation.

Lynch, Marta (Argentina, 1929–1985). Novelist and short-story writer of strong political convictions. Her first novel dealt with the rise to power of an Argentine president, *La alfombra roja* (1963); her second, with corruption in the army, *Al vencedor* (1965). Among her later novels are *La Señora Ordoñez* (1968), *Los años de fuego* (1980), and *El cruce del río* (1972), which was banned by the military government.

Ocampo, Silvina (Argentina, 1906–). Painter, poet, and short-story writer. Her books include *Viaje olvidado* (1937), *Los sonetos del jardín* (1946), *Poemas de amor desesperado* (1949), *Amarillo celeste* (1972), *Autobiografía de Irene* (1948), *La Furia* (1959), *Las invitadas* (1961), and *Los días de la noche* (1970). With her husband, Adolfo Bioy Casares, she wrote a detective novel, *Los que aman, odian* (1947).

Pizarnik, Alejandra (Argentina, 1936–1972). Poet greatly influenced by William Blake and the French surrealists. Her books include *La tierra más ajena* (1955), *La última inocencia* (1956), *Las aventuras perdidas* (1958), *Arbol de Diana* (1962), *Los Trabajos y las noches* (1965), *Extracción de la piedra de locura* (1968), and *El infierno musical* (1972).

Poniatowska, Elena (France, 1923–   ). Journalist, novelist, and short-story writer, she came to Mexico at the age of ten with her father, a Polish nobleman. Her books combine the style of investigative journalism with the imagination of a fiction writer. Her most important novel to date is *Hasta no verte, Jesús mío* (1952). One of her earlier books, *Todo empezó en domingo* (1965) has been translated as *Massacre in Mexico* (1971).

Queiroz, Rachel de (Brazil, 1910–   ). Novelist and short-story writer. In 1931 she joined the Communist Party, from which she was expelled in 1933. Her novels defy the classic convention of the submissive woman and portray instead compassionate and intelligent heroines. Among the most important are *O Quinze* (1930), *Caminho de Pedras* (1937), and *As Três Marias* (1937). Her short stories were collected in *Cem Crônicas Selecionadas* (1958).

Silveira de Queiroz, Dinah (Brazil, 1911–   ). Novelist and short-story writer, she was the first woman to be awarded the Machado de Assis Prize given by the Brazilian Academy of Letters. She is the author of *Comba Malina* (1939) and *As Noites do Morro do Encanto* (1957). She has also written books for children and plays.

Somers, Armonía (Uruguay, 1918–   ). Under her real name, Armonía Etchepare de Henestrosa, she has written several books on teaching. Her first novel, *La mujer desnuda*, appeared in 1950. Her collected stories were published by Angel Rama in 1968.

Guido Almansi & Claude Béguin
Theatre of Sleep: An Anthology of Literary Dreams
£10.95

'The ultimate bedside book . . . good for 1001 white nights'
Peter Conrad, Observer Books of the Year

Bringing together a wide selection of dreams drawn from the literature of all ages and many cultures, from Aristotle and Apollinaire to Bob Dylan, Proust, Vonnegut and Wagner, some of which have been translated into English for the first time, with every piece put in its literary and historical context, this is a hugely entertaining work of some of the most bizarre, imaginative and perplexing passages ever written.

'As the immense richness of the dreams in this excellent collection demonstrates, no theory ever seems likely to account for those strange safaris on which each of us sets out every night across the width of our heads . . . Their anthology never wearies . . . I finished (it) feeling marvellously relaxed' *J. G. Ballard, Guardian*

'Their range is vast' *Anthony Storr, Sunday Times*

'A polished performance . . . *Theatre of Sleep* entices us into a hinterland between the unconscious and the highly self-conscious though taking care not to parade the expected and the obvious. The choice of material has been eclectic and, occasionally, esoteric. It's purpose, a just one, is to remind today's reader that although dreams may no longer exist for him as carriers of portents and messages – other than, perhaps, sexual ones – they are still as much an influence on the writer's imagination as they ever were'
Ronald Blythe, Sunday Telegraph

'A vivid tapestry of the uncontrolled imagination' *Women's Review*

'Well done' *Anthony Powell, Daily Telegraph*

edited by Alberto Manguel
Black Water £4.95
the anthology of fantastic literature

Here in this huge anthology is a kaleidoscope of brilliant writing from the Magi
of the imagination. Alberto Manguel has selected seventy-two tales –
including possibly the shortest fantastic story in the world – from life on the
edge of the twilight zone. Stories from Herman Hesse, Bruno Schultz, Italo
Calvino, Vladimir Nabokov, Jorge-Luis Borges, Franz Kafka and many, many
more: irresistible masterpieces, many of which are appearing for the first
time in the English language.

'Fantastic literature makes use of our everyday world as a façade through
which the undefinable appears, hinting at the half-forgotten dreams of our
imagination . . . the impossible seeping into the possible, what Wallace
Stevens calls "black water breaking into reality" ' *Alberto Manguel*

All these books are available at your local bookshop or newsagent, or
can be ordered direct from the publisher. Indicate the number of
copies required and fill in the form below

....

Name_____
(Block letters please)

Address_____

_____

Send to CS Department, Pan Books Ltd, PO Box 40, Basingstoke, Hants
Please enclose remittance to the value of the cover price plus:
60p for the first book plus 30p per copy for each additional book ordered
to a maximum charge of £2.40 to cover postage and packing
Applicable only in the UK

While every effort is made to keep prices low, it is sometimes
necessary to increase prices at short notice. Pan Books reserve
the right to show on covers and charge new retail prices which
may differ from those advertised in the text or elsewhere